T0372934

Looked After

Looked After

A Childhood in Care

Ashley John-Baptiste

**HODDER &
STOUGHTON**

First published in Great Britain in 2024 by Hodder & Stoughton Limited
An Hachette UK company

4

Copyright © Ashley John-Baptiste 2024

The right of Ashley John-Baptiste to be identified as the Author of the Work has been
asserted by him in accordance with the Copyright, Designs and Patents Act 1988.

A CIP catalogue record for this title is available from the British Library

Hardback ISBN 9781399711920
ebook ISBN 9781399711944

Typeset in Celeste MT by Manipal Technologies Limited

Printed and bound in Great Britain by Clays Ltd, Elcograf S.p.A.

Hodder & Stoughton policy is to use papers that are natural, renewable
and recyclable products and made from wood grown in sustainable forests.
The logging and manufacturing processes are expected to conform
to the environmental regulations of the country of origin.

Hodder & Stoughton Limited
Carmelite House
50 Victoria Embankment
London EC4Y 0DZ

www.hodder.co.uk

To my girls – Joanna, Zoe and Mia.

Thank you for being the family my younger
self could only dream of. x

AUTHOR'S NOTE

If you had told me when I was sixteen that I'd go on to become a BBC journalist and broadcaster, a dad and a husband, I would have thought you were smoking a recreational drug.

So often, as a kid, I grappled with the immediacy of survival. I was caught up in a web of confusion about my identity as a foster kid and, at times, held no hope for my future. My life now is considerably different from how it was at the start, but still, the wounds of my childhood linger. As I frequently observe the childhood bliss that my infant daughters enjoy, it chills me to think that when I was their age, I had already been placed in care with key familial bonds shattered.

I have presented documentaries and reports about the children's care system across Britain that have required me to share bits of my own story. But I have never looked back on the first eighteen years of my life with the attention that writing this book has demanded of me.

This isn't a memoir in the purest sense. I'm thirty-four, with a lot of life to still live, hopefully. Rather, this is a book specifically about my life as a looked-after child. I hope that sharing my experiences gives you, the reader, an insight into what it can be like to grow up in care.

To write this book, I had to rediscover the voice of my inner child. I had to remember and re-feel past moments, trauma and events as best as I could. I had to write with integrity, and unfiltered perspective.

Certain moments that I recount in these pages may have been perceived differently by the various people involved at any given time. And in any scenario of my childhood, a range of factors could have been at play that I didn't know about at the time. It's clear that looked-after children don't get to see or understand the full context of their lives in care; and the system doesn't offer insights into them.

But with all of that said, this book is simply about my take, as a child navigating a system. I have changed names and sometimes places to protect the identities of those involved. At times, I have referred to the social-services records from my time in care. That allowed me to corroborate timings and events. Fundamentally, however, this is a raw, honest account of a childhood in care.

A lot has been said about the care system and looked-after children, yet little of the existing literature is written by people with first-hand involvement. So the best thing I can do is honour my own experiences and feelings, giving them the most transparent expression possible.

I truly hope you learn something from my story.

I

FAMILIAL

It all begins with Joyce.

I can't remember anyone before her, although my records mention an emergency foster family I was placed with at about the age of two.

Apparently, Joyce became my foster mum when I was around four years old, but when I think back to the start of my life she is all I can remember. They, whoever they are, say that one way of coping with childhood trauma is by forgetting. Maybe that's me.

'Foster mum' isn't an accurate term for Joyce. She was the benevolent Caribbean grandmother that anyone would love to have in their life.

Joyce exuded wisdom and strength. With a thick Jamaican accent and celebrity-like status in her community of Walworth, south London, she was in her sixties when she took me in. She was, undeniably, a local legend. She had fostered many children before me. But I knew I was special to her. I was more than fostered. More than looked after.

'Ashley, you is me likkle boy,' she'd say fondly and regularly in her Jamaican patois.

A Black woman, Joyce had striking blue-brown eyes and was known for her signature headscarf. Although she sometimes relied on a walking stick because of a dodgy kneecap, she had boundless energy and a strong frame.

We lived in a small, cosy three-bedroom house just off Walworth Road. It was a council house, but for me, back then, it could have been a mansion in Chelsea. It had everything I needed. It was home.

More than just a revolving door for the countless foster kids Joyce took in, her home bustled with people all the time. Joyce was visited almost daily by her biological adult children – two daughters and a son (Keisha, Porsha and Daryl), her grandchildren and a flurry of neighbours, friends and locals.

Joyce was the centre of her community. Whether it was for a dose of timely wisdom, a nostalgic story about her early life in Jamaica or some hearty Caribbean food, someone was always at Joyce's door. Her home was a sanctuary for so many.

The scent of her rice and peas and well-seasoned chicken was ever-present, synonymous with my earliest memories. Likewise, the American-country sounds of Jim Reeves music playing in the background while she polished her ornaments and plumped her sofa are among the primary normalcies of my childhood.

I suppose I can't remember when I first knew that I was 'looked after', but the unavoidable trappings of being in care – such as children moving in and out and the regular visits from social workers – confirmed there was more baggage to my life with Joyce than I wanted.

But for the most part, I loved life there.

Joyce's family was my family. Her daughter Keisha had a son called Conor. He was my constant companion. We were the same age, and he'd come round daily and sleep over most weekends. I was light-skinned like him. We were inseparable.

'Those cuties are gonna be trouble when they're older!' our neighbour Shirley would fondly tell Joyce whenever she saw us together in our small front garden.

Although we were the same age, I looked up to Conor. Even as a young kid, he seemed to exude security and self-confidence. He was a pillar of strength. More like a big brother.

Our antics consisted of play fights around the house, kickabouts in the garden and regular trips to the local adventure playground and youth club. As we got a bit older, that's where we learned to play table tennis – a game that secured our bond as brothers.

Another highlight? Saturdays. That's when Joyce would take us to East Street Market. 'Make sure you stay close to me in these crowds, you hear?' Joyce would shout to us through the hustle and bustle of the market chaos.

There, she'd buy fresh meat and vegetables for her recipes. During those trips, she'd always get side-tracked by a conversation or three as she bumped into locals. And in those moments, Conor and I would get up to our own mischief. Market trips would be topped off with a cheap toy from a stall and 20p's worth of pick 'n' mix from Dalston's Local – the neighbourhood off-licence.

For me, those market trips and pick 'n' mix treats with Conor were moments of sheer joy. I needed no convincing that I was at home. And even if the boring social-worker meetings that often popped up alluded to a more complicated story about my family, for me it was simple: with Joyce, I was at home.

Perhaps peak season at Joyce's was Christmas.

Given the boundless community and cuisine in Joyce's house, Christmas was an occasion she excelled at. Throw in her strong Christian faith alongside that, and she became almost evangelical in her aim to make sure everyone in the community felt included and fed at that time of year.

I would have been around six years old when, like most kids, all I wanted for Christmas was a Nintendo Game Boy. I pleaded with Joyce: 'Please can I get one?' I begged in my infant tone. But there was no verbal response, just a stern look through her thick-rimmed glasses.

Joyce received money from the local authority for looking after me, but she must have also gone into her own pocket when it came to the gifts she bought me. Even so, she soon broke the news to me that a Game Boy was too expensive a present that year. I sighed in disappointment. It was all we kids wanted back then, and I had hoped that somehow Joyce would come through. But she didn't budge.

I remember so much of that Christmas.

On Christmas day, I awoke early and opened the curtains with boyish excitement. Even at that early hour, the smell of Joyce's cooking drifted upstairs to our bedroom. She was always joyously militant in preparing the festivities from early in the morning.

I reckon that at Joyce's, I felt like a normal child at Christmas. I remember the overwhelming sense of excitement for the presents and food. I even looked forward to seeing who would turn up at Joyce's door.

Keisha and Conor arrived that particular Christmas morning, not long after I had got up. Joyce plied us kids (there were two other foster children living with her at the time; I shared a bunk bed with one of them) with fried bacon, scrambled eggs, beans and toast. She was at her best when feeding and serving others.

Throughout the morning, Christmas telly, the clanging of Joyce's cooking and general chit-chat permeated the house. After breakfast, we made up as much fun as we could, although deep down we were all waiting for the green light to open presents. It was all about the presents in those days. Eventually, Conor, me and the two other children were let loose on them.

The tree, every year, was always packed with gifts. In the weeks leading up to Christmas day, scores of people would pass through, inevitably also delivering a gift or two. Toy cars, football stickers, chocolate and socks were the usual fare. But as I tore through wrapping paper and some well-received gifts, there was no sign of a Game Boy. No sign of that weighty, rectangular block in gift wrap.

Joyce and Keisha fondly watched us from the sofa as we crawled around the tree on all fours. I think Joyce got as much joy as we did just from watching us.

'Careful, Conor,' Keisha occasionally cautioned her son, attempting to quell the chaos.

Following weeks of anticipation, it took barely an instant to unwrap and tear through the multitude of gifts. And then . . .

'I got one,' shouted Conor.

I beheld it in his hands. A shiny, new Nintendo Game Boy. I tried to hide the emerging disappointment.

Soon enough I had unwrapped all my presents and, as Joyce had tried to warn me . . . there was no Game Boy. Even then, though, I knew enough to be grateful all the same. But despite my best efforts at hiding my feelings – my hopes for a Christmas topped off with a Nintendo Game Boy now gone – I'm sure everyone could see how gutted I was. Most notably Conor.

'Ash, don't worry. You can share with me,' he exclaimed, still jubilant over his gift.

At some point, not too long after the unwrapping of presents, Joyce suddenly darted out of the living room, then walked back in, hands behind her back. She looked at me with deep fondness in her eyes.

'You know you will always be family, Ashley. You know that, right?'

Her warm Jamaican tone was like a mug of hot chocolate. I always felt reassured by it and knew she'd have my back, no matter what.

I must have been nodding when she brought something out from behind her back.

I looked at her eagerly. 'A Game Boy!' I exclaimed. I turned to Conor. The two of us bobbed up and down, giddy with excitement. There were peals of laughter as I uttered abundant thanks to Joyce.

'I love you,' she said to me as she looked at me deeply, as if I was the only one in the room. As if *I* was all that mattered. And I believed her.

I never fully appreciated the significance of those words back then. I heard them often, and any time I drifted towards feeling like I didn't belong, she'd always convince me otherwise.

So it was the perfect Christmas morning. And as morning turned to afternoon, the whole of Joyce's family turned up. Then there were the others – an assortment of neighbours and church friends, who'd pass through, all in a bid to show some goodwill (and grab a plate of Joyce's cooking, no doubt).

Christmas crackers, a staple Eddie Murphy film, family games and the Christmas special of *Top of the Pops*, all combined to make the perfect Christmas. And by the time we had finished dinner – a spread of jerk chicken, curried goat, rice and peas, with turkey and all the trimmings – we couldn't possibly have wanted for anything else. Childhood bliss.

As it grew dark outside, during the evening of this special Christmas day, Joyce had one more surprise for me.

She beckoned me upstairs as the rest of the gang cosied up in the living room watching Christmas telly. She stood in my bedroom clutching a black bin bag. I was curious.

'Ashley, I have something to tell you . . .'

I looked at her, unsure of what to make of the moment. I'd never seen Joyce show even a slight sign of nerves. Until now.

'Ashley, your mother stopped by late last night while you were asleep. She wanted to give you these Christmas presents . . .'

With care and gentleness, she slowly handed me the black bin bag. I looked inside. There was a portable stereo, toy cars and other gifts. All for me? Everything looked so expensive – like the presents rich kids receive in the movies.

I didn't know much about my mother and this was the first time Joyce had mentioned anything about knowing or being in touch with her. At that point, I didn't think about the details of how, or why, Joyce knew my mum. Clearly, social services hadn't connected them; it hadn't been mentioned at our recent meeting. But in that moment, I wasn't preoccupied with questions about what could have happened to my mum for me to end up in care.

Retrospectively, I am not confident that Joyce was even allowed to have contact with my mum in this sort of way or have her send stuff to me. Was she allowed to mediate a connection between her foster son and his biological mother? Was she allowed to play such a sensitive role and risk damaging things between me and my mother for the long haul? Surely, she was violating the rules set by the powerful courts and social workers?

In any event, that bin bag marked the first, albeit indirect, encounter with my biological mother that I can remember.

'And there's one more thing . . .' Joyce added. 'Your mum wanted you to have this photo of her.'

Joyce extended her hand and I took the small paper print from it. It wasn't much bigger than a passport photo and showed the face of a young, pretty, smiling blonde woman. That was it. I was seeing what my mum looked like for the first time as a looked-after child. Thing is, though, it was just a picture. It didn't come with a hug, or an 'I've always loved you, Ashley'. Just a photo. Still, it was more than I'd had a few moments earlier.

Joyce said she was pretty, like an angel. I could see that, too.

In that moment, my appreciation of the cool gifts from my mum outweighed any deep curiosity I had about my family backstory. Priorities would no doubt change, but for now, Joyce and the gang were still my family. They were all that mattered. A late-night intrusion by a black bag and photo wasn't going to convince me otherwise.

Looking back, I wonder what Joyce made of my reaction to the photo. Perhaps it wasn't what she expected? Perhaps it was not quite the moment she was building it up to be – or hoping it would be.

Was Joyce aware that to me, she was all I needed? Did she know she would be my forever home?

I soon scurried back downstairs to join Conor and play Mario Kart on my new Game Boy. What a Christmas.

My bond with Joyce felt strong. She would say I had a sixth sense for when she was vulnerable – something I took great pride in.

According to one of Joyce's many stories, she was once in the bathroom upstairs, feeling faint. I was downstairs. She barely whispered my name – but still – I ran upstairs in a hurry, ready and eager to help her in any way possible. There was an unspoken connection between the two of us. Like a puppy, I was her loyal defender, willing to do anything for her. Joyce was there for me and I'd always be there for her. But despite the faith I put in Joyce, it seemed she was intent on subtly directing me to the other 'real' family I but had known nothing about.

The photo Joyce gave me of my biological mother was the only trace I had of her for years. In my early years at primary school, I would brandish it around the playground, often boasting about how pretty my mother was.

'Look what I've got!' I'd shout to whoever cared to listen, frantically waving the photo, exclaiming to uninterested kids that the person in the photo was where I got my good looks from. After all, I had no idea what my dad looked like.

The more I became aware of other children's parents and their 'normal' families, the more relieved I became that I had a photo. My proof that I had a mum.

Some kids carry teddy bears or toy cars wherever they go. I carried my photo. It was my one and only prop to convince the other school kids that I wasn't a reject.

One day, however, that photo disappeared. I was at school, playing with other kids in the playground during break time. Running around in a frenzy, I didn't realise I'd dropped the photo. Nearby, meanwhile, the school caretaker was milling around with a street vacuum, cleaning the school grounds. In the blink of an eye, completely unaware, he'd hoovered over the picture.

I watched as his machine swept over it. I looked up at the caretaker – he was completely oblivious to what he'd done. It was gone. Despite me asking him to get my photo from his machine, he never did retrieve it from the vacuum bag. One boy's treasure, another man's trash.

I went home deflated that day. I knew no one at school would understand what the loss of that photo meant. I never told Joyce.

While the photo, over time, would gain a deeper significance in my mind and eventually spark my curiosity about who my mum really was, the only other insight I was given into her came from my biological uncle who began to visit me a couple of years into life at Joyce's.

Uncle Terry, my mother's brother, lived in the same part of London as me and was eventually given permission by social services to visit once a month. I remember a bit about him. Pale. Foggy glasses and greasy hair. He didn't appear to hold by the sort of hygiene rules that Joyce worked so hard to instil in me.

Terry wasn't employed. I always just seemed to know that. He mentioned that he'd once tried his hand at working in a nursery, but that eventually fell through. He lived in a council flat by himself. A self-confessed loner. No friends or partner.

I think visiting me was less about his concern for my welfare than relieving his own sense of loneliness. Still, I liked my time with him. Any time he visited, he'd come armed with treats for me – a *Beano* comic book and a Mars bar.

It was on one occasion when he took me to the local McDonald's that I formed the next impression of who my mother was.

Terry and my mother hadn't got on, and they'd also spent time in the care system as children. I was, therefore, part of a cycle of intergenerational care. My mother had me when she was a teenager. My dad was much older. My uncle said something along the lines of my mum not having made the best choices.

The more time I spent with my uncle, the more he fed me negative stories, and the more Joyce would tell me positive things about my mum. It was as if she sensed the negative spin my uncle was feeding me about my mother. According to Joyce, my mum had a good heart. She said that my mum called her regularly to check on how I was doing. But she never mentioned this to social services during our awkward meetings.

Joyce told me that my mum cared about me. She even promised that one day, I would get to meet her. Through Joyce's observations about my mother, I built up an almost mythical image of who she was. And over time, the few impressions I'd formed of my mum – through the long-gone photo, Joyce and my uncle – sparked a deeper curiosity.

Just as Joyce was the first foster parent I could remember, Karen was the first social worker.

Karen was a white woman with a large frame and long black hair and a face that carried a softness that felt maternal at first glance. But, to me, there was also a coldness. As my social worker, she'd visit Joyce's home every few months to 'assess how the placement was progressing', to put it in her words. She was always armed with a pen, notepad and bag brimming with paperwork. Part of her role was to make sure I was getting on okay.

Whenever she visited, she'd get out some sort of form, where she'd tick boxes and write copious notes. I couldn't put my finger on why, but I never felt fully at ease around Karen. Did she really care about me? That was a question I'd ask myself. I suspected that I was probably just one of many kids she had to visit and fill in forms about. Even with that caring, maternal veneer, I wasn't convinced. She seemed too busy, too professional, to be able to care properly.

When she came to visit, I always felt as if I was under scrutiny. I felt a gaze of judgement. And during our meetings, I was always performative, putting on a fake front.

There was an unspoken pact with Joyce when it came to these social-services meetings. I was to act as if all was perfect in the world. We couldn't give social services any reason to believe I needed to be moved on.

I always found it a bit funny that, in front of social workers, Joyce would try to sound posh and water down her Jamaican dialect.

'Would you like a cup of tea, Karen?' she'd say in a most awkward fashion, exaggerating her smile and over-enunciating. But Joyce was perfect to me. She didn't need to put on a show.

Karen didn't say much to me during her visits, but her gaze spoke volumes. And, in time, I would realise why.

2

A CONSEQUENCE

A few years into life at Joyce's, when I was around seven years old, Karen seemed to sense the growing questions I had about my mum and suggested it was time for me to find out more about my life story.

What did she mean by my 'life story'? She explained that over a series of meetings, she would work with another professional from the council to explain bits of my family background to me – issues relating to my biological family and why I was put into the care system.

Those meetings were held at McDonald's with Karen and the male professional in question. I wasn't entirely sure about his job title. I knew he wasn't a social worker like Karen, but he still carried that professional manner that, to me, made him feel entirely unrelatable. He took notes and seemed to speak down to me – all the stuff that reeked of a social-care professional. During those meetings, Happy Meal cheeseburgers and milkshakes were spliced with veiled hints at the vulnerabilities my mother faced as a young mum. Maybe the vanilla milkshakes were meant to wash down the gut-wrenching blows of neglect and confusion I often felt during those 'sessions'. I would also occasionally be encouraged to draw pictures about the perceptions I had of my family.

Karen kept a digital record of the conversations and drawings, and after a few weeks of meetings, she gave me a floppy disk titled, 'Ashley's Life Story'. That was it. My early childhood was now embodied in a floppy disk. No cherished memories or warm stories. No photo of my birth; no warm recollections about my temperament as a baby; no childhood toys. No cute video clips. Just a floppy disk of cold, hard information.

The details from my life-story sessions with the social workers sparked more questions than answers. There were no details about whether I had siblings, no information about my father. Nothing. And for all the stuff that was being recorded about my mum, I didn't even know what she sounded like. With the lack of information available, I had just a thin patch-work of insight into myself – nothing that told me who I really was.

Perhaps the biggest takeaway from my life-story work was discovering that I was mixed race. My mother was white-British; my father Black-Dominican. It explained the puffy, curly hair that grew when it got long enough without me getting a trim.

The one thing I knew as fact was that Joyce loved me. And even with all my surfacing questions about my identity, she was all that really mattered. So long as I had Joyce, I knew I would be okay.

For as far back as I can remember, school was a melting pot of contradictions for me.

My first school was Falondale Primary. It was a place I was unprepared for. As a boy, I was dysfunctional and ill-equipped to muster the discipline needed to get through classes and complete basic tasks. I didn't trust teachers. How the hell was I supposed to trust them, or adults at all? None of them really cared. Joyce was the only one I could rely on.

At the same time, though, school occasionally felt like a place of escapism; somewhere I had equal standing with the other kids. On the school playground, or during an English test, I wasn't a foster kid. I was equal and able to perform to the same level as any other child.

That's why, for all the challenges that school presented me with, on some level, I enjoyed it. And even if I struggled in a variety of ways, deep down I embraced the normality of the institution. So it was the secret affection I had for school that made one particular day all the more regrettable.

I was around seven years old.

Despite my default position of mistrust, I had taken a liking to my year-two teacher, Mrs Oke. She seemed brilliantly clever and caring, with a Nigerian dialect and warmth that made even the most vulnerable, reclusive child feel safe. She seemed to get on well with Joyce, too. Many afternoons, on picking me up from school, Joyce would chat with Mrs Oke on the school playground. In those moments, she didn't turn on her posh dialect like she did with Karen, the social worker. She was herself, with full Jamaican patois. She seemed to enjoy those conversations.

After the morning break on *that* day, it was time for an arts-and-crafts lesson. I often sat with my classmate Sam for those activities. As Mrs Oke set out a creative task for the lesson, I loosely took in the instructions between fussing around and, typically, being a distraction. (Even back then, I thrived on attention.)

In a rapid flurry of developments, I got into a scuffle with Sam. We started bickering, and before I knew it, I had punched him in the face.

'Ouch! Mrs Oke!' he blurted out in mild agony, before turning bright red and starting to cry infant tears.

Incidents like these always escalated far too quickly, before I could grasp the effect I was having. I had never learned how to control my emotions and navigate mainstream social scenarios, and in my boyish flare-ups, impulse often got the better, so that even the smallest conflict or confrontation could spark the short fuse of my unruly temper. But as Sam began to cry, I knew I had taken it too far.

'I'm sorry, it was an accident,' I called out in panic.

'That's it, Ashley, you're off to the head teacher's office. Now!' she said. (When Mrs Oke took a serious tone, her Nigerian accent would be even more evident.)

'No miss, please . . . It was an accident!'

On some level, it genuinely was. I hadn't meant to hurt Sam. But Mrs Oke wasn't having any of it.

I began to get worked up in a fit of anxiety and tantrum, and within moments, a teaching assistant was escorting me to the head teacher's office. I started to kick and scream and shout, adamant that I wanted to be back in the domain of Mrs Oke. She was the only one who had any chance of calming me down now.

My temper mounted to a crescendo, but next thing I knew, I was in the head teacher's office, and he was looking down at me disapprovingly. This wasn't the first time I had been sent to him for my behaviour. His room, lined with cabinets, files and paperwork, was in stark contrast to the colour and creativity of Mrs Oke's classroom. The multicoloured displays in her classroom sparked an ambience of fun and play. This sombre office, however, screamed punishment.

The head insisted I calm down. 'Okay, Ashley. That's enough. Stop,' he said firmly.

I refused. Why should I submit to his authority?

Instantly, he threatened me with suspension if I didn't acquiesce. If that was a threat, it was a pathetic one. It couldn't quieten me. If Mrs Oke couldn't settle me, this dickhead couldn't. My heart began to beat faster, all sense of control evaporating. I just wanted out of his office.

'Let me go!' I shouted.

I began to bang on his door and scream with as much volume as I could muster.

He raised his voice, attempting to quell the infant tantrum before him.

That compelled me to rage through his cabinets, ripping through his important-looking files and neatly collated paperwork.

I had crossed a line.

'Heather, can you come quickly?' he called out, breathless, popping his head out of his office to summon his assistant.

'On my way,' she called from up the hallway.

Within moments, the headmaster and his assistant had forcefully carried me out of the office and – after what felt like a lifetime of shouting and protesting – out of the school. They had decided, in an instant, to physically carry me home to Joyce's, just a short walk away.

With puffy red faces, struggling to contain me, the head and his assistant carried me as I kicked and screamed and people on the streets looked on.

'LET ME GO,' I shouted.

'Ashley, this just has to stop. You're not doing yourself any favours here!' said the head, battling to hold me as I violently attempted to free myself from their grip. But soon enough, out of breath, they'd brought me to my front door.

Joyce opened the door swiftly and greeted them with that fake and forced posh tone.

The school must have called her in advance. 'Hello, sir,' she said. 'I am so sorry for this . . .'

She continued to profusely apologise for my behaviour, and in between engaging them, gave me a quick, sharp look that told me she was livid. Instantly, I piped down. I knew I was in trouble now.

Joyce then bid them off and closed the door.

Inside . . . silence. Silence was always the clearest marker that Joyce was genuinely unhappy.

Time went by.

It felt like hours before she spoke with me about the reports of my behaviour. Clearly, ripping up the head's paperwork was more of an affront than punching Sam in the face. After all, that was what sparked his decision to physically escort me home.

Joyce sent me to my room.

Just a few hours after me being dropped home, the house telephone rang. It was school. I was to stay at home and not attend school until further notice. I can still remember the disappointment in Joyce's eyes as she passed on the school's message. She didn't shout at me or make threats to punish me. Her tired demeanour was perhaps the most saddening aspect of the whole furore.

I hated it when I disappointed Joyce. I hated it when my lack of self-discipline overrode my good intentions. I only ever wanted to please Joyce. I could suck up her anger or frustration any day, but seeing her upset was a pill too bitter to stomach.

I told myself I'd try harder when I went back to school. I presumed I'd be off for the rest of the week and that I'd be able to go back the following one.

That wasn't the case.

A couple of mornings after the incident, Joyce received a letter from school informing her that I wasn't allowed to attend the school again. I was permanently excluded.

I'm not sure I fully understood what she was saying. It was a shock, to say the least.

Seven was extremely young to get kicked out of a school. I thought about my friends. Sam . . . Leanne. The dazzling colours of Mrs Oke's classroom flashed through my brain. I thought about football during playtime . . . the normality of sitting in the classroom as we were read a story . . . the school playground, where I lost the photo of my mum. Like that photo, it was all gone now.

What would Mrs Oke say about my expulsion? Did she agree? To me, it felt wrong. Unfair. But then again, to them – understandably, I guess – I was a problem child. Fostered. Undisciplined. Even at seven, a lost cause.

While my child brain couldn't grasp even a fraction of the implications of what exclusion meant, I knew it wasn't good news. I knew that I had really let Joyce down. And what would her family say when she told them? What would Karen say? She'd definitely find out.

I can't remember Joyce shouting once about my exclusion. Her reaction was perhaps the hardest part.

Exclusion felt like rejection. At both school and home. I was convinced that I was too much of a burden.

Looking back, I wonder if the head teacher ever wondered what sort of message a school exclusion would send to a seven-year-old foster boy. Was it meant to help me? I wasn't good enough to remain a part of that school community. The exclusion was proof that I was abnormal, unable to function in a normal setting. I was, after all, looked after.

Over the following days and weeks, the shock of the news of exclusion morphed into a deep sadness. Nobody seemed to want me. Well, apart from Joyce. That was something to be comforted by.

An overconsumption of children's telly and helping Joyce with chores now filled my days. Then Karen, the social worker, came to visit. Although I never really enjoyed hearing from my social worker, I thought this meeting would be a standard procedure. Social workers must visit when significant developments occur in the placement of a foster child. That meant, to me, that they had to look like they cared. Maybe she did. Maybe my cynicism was misplaced.

Karen decided to take me out for a walk, while Joyce stayed at home, and I assumed she wanted to discuss the expulsion with me. She bought me an ice cream en route, but despite the pleasantries, I guessed that Karen had ultimately come here to judge me.

Her words felt punitive. I was reminded that I had let everyone down. And I was ruining things for myself, she emphasised.

I was normally quite placid with Karen. This occasion was no different. I knew I wasn't good enough, perhaps even a failure. And she confirmed that. But I certainly wasn't prepared for what she said next.

'Ashley, Joyce and I have been speaking about your future. There's no easy way of saying this, but we've decided it's time for you to leave this placement and move somewhere else.'

Sitting down on a bench in a park, mid-afternoon, everything around me faded. There's no way I would have processed those words straight away. I was being made to leave Joyce's?

My mind tried to fight back. This couldn't have been Karen's decision to make and there was surely no way Joyce would want me to leave her. She always told me she loved me and that I was family.

I sat there, not entirely sure if what Karen said was an immutable fact or just some professional speak. Joyce was like my mum and nan all wrapped in one. I knew she'd have my back and quickly reject Karen's suggestion. Family fights for family. Nevertheless, Karen's words transported me to a limbo state of numbness.

After a while, she walked me back to Joyce's. I followed along, ready for Joyce to vindicate me.

Joyce led us to the living room. Karen's tea was already awaiting her next to the sofa. It was as if Joyce knew how everything was going to unfold. Was this all pre-planned?

As Joyce, Karen and I sat together, the initial silence lasted a lifetime. I felt numb. My eyes turned to Joyce with a desperate plea and powerlessness. I can't remember her looking back at me. In fact, she must've looked down at her hands for the majority of that meeting.

Sitting in that living room – *my* living room – that moment felt like an eternity. Karen rehashed what she had explained to me in the park. She emphasised it was something Joyce had agreed to. Really? But was it Karen's idea? I'd never know.

I kept looking back at Joyce with urgency. She looked down firmly. Do something, Joyce! I thought to myself. But all Joyce did during Karen's monologue was occasionally nod and murmur in agreement.

Karen's tone was gentle, yet every word pierced like a blade. Then, soon enough, she put down her empty teacup, spoke some bullshit platitudes and left.

'I'll be in touch once I have more information about your next placement,' she said as she exited the front door. Not your normal goodbye. She had just launched a grenade and left before having to deal with the collateral damage.

The one thing I knew from the living-room chat was that both Joyce and Karen were on the same page. Joyce seemed to be on board with this decision.

I didn't really talk to Joyce about it. After that meeting, I didn't plead. Maybe I was too stunned. I went to my room. That's where the tears fell. I stared at that magnolia bedroom wall for ages. The details of Joyce's home that I so easily took for granted – her lace curtains, my bedroom carpet, the cupboard door I so often slammed – would soon all be gone. A string of foster children had come and gone during my time at Joyce's, but I never expected that I would be one of them. I now felt disposable.

Joyce had often called me her family, but now I felt she clearly couldn't have meant it. Was it because of the expulsion? Maybe my tantrums? Why was Joyce letting me go? Maybe she had been lying to me all this time. I wasn't her family. She didn't love me. How could she possibly love me *and* let me go? Maybe foster carers were trained to say that sort of crap, even if they don't mean it.

I thought about Conor, Keisha – the whole family. I'd be letting them all go, too. Where would I live? The weight of Karen's words paralysed me inside.

The cadence of my despair was broken when Keisha rang the doorbell. She had popped over with Conor for dinner. As we all ate in the living room, I didn't protest. On the surface, it was business as usual. That's what hurt the most. The news, the TV soaps, Keisha sharing her opinion on everything and, as normal, I went off and played with Conor. I didn't tell him we didn't have much time left to play together.

Because I wasn't given a date for when I'd be leaving Joyce's, some part of me hoped I could persuade her to keep me. I determined that I would start a campaign of perfect behaviour. I'd become more lovable. That way, Joyce would remember I was her son, and that she loved me. She would decide, I prayed, that I could stay with her, after all. (Blimey. Why should a child ever have to think like that?)

And as days passed, things seemed to subtly slip back into normality. Food, family, music. The only difference was that I'd spend the school days at home. Once I was kicked out of primary school, another school wasn't found for me.

The morning my life changed came unannounced, although maybe I should have clocked it given all the excessive laundry Joyce was doing.

It felt like any other lovely spring morning with Joyce. I sat in front of the TV, eating Cheerios and watching children's programmes. Joyce scurried around the living room, polishing ornaments, as the smell of her early-morning cooking preparations filled the house. I was, even if only briefly, content.

There was a knock at the door. Which of Joyce's friends would it be today? She answered the door. There was no normal cheery greeting from a neighbour or friend. Instead, people I had never seen before walked into the living room – a Black man with a muscular frame and dreadlocks and, with him, some inconspicuous-looking professional. Karen followed behind.

Sat crossed-legged on the floor with children's telly blaring in the background, I turned my head to behold these strange new adults towering over me.

This was it, then. The moment I was dreading had finally arrived. My stomach plummeted. I began to despair. I felt deeply helpless.

With sensitivity but also caution, Karen began to explain that the time had come for me to leave Joyce's. She needn't have said anything.

Like a new baby pleading for its mother's milk, I began to cry out for Joyce.

She didn't respond. In fact, she wasn't in the room at this point. She had gone to pack me a suitcase.

I ran out of the living room and upstairs, weeping for Joyce. I had no time for bravado in that moment. Fear and desperation broke out within me.

'Please don't kick me out,' I begged Joyce, my arms outstretched to her for comfort.

Joyce was busy packing, and barely made eye contact with me. This hurt bad. I shouted out pledges to her that I'd be better behaved. I could be whatever she wanted me to be, so long as she didn't let me go.

Joyce had never explained why I had to go. Karen had broken the news and no explanation had since been given. Maybe Joyce was ill? If so, I deserved to know. But right now I was too consumed with begging to ask 'Why?'

As she finished packing my suitcase, my cries turned to screams. Shrieks of fear. Fear of abandonment. I refused to go downstairs.

'Ashley, this is for your own good,' Joyce said gently. Wearily.

Still refusing to go downstairs, and sobbing, I clung tightly on to a bunk-bed leg, as if for dear life. From downstairs, Karen shouted up for me to come down. She reiterated that the decision was final. Cold. Then, eventually, she came upstairs with the two workers, who I'd later find out were from the place I was moving to.

I couldn't have cared less. I had no shame, just desperation. 'I'm not going,' I shouted. 'NO!'

I ran to the bedroom window, sat on the ledge and threatened to jump out if they didn't leave me alone. There was no way I'd have jumped out of a first-floor window, but it was all I had – a futile threat, rooted in desperation. And deep down, I knew any attempt to resist leaving was meaningless.

Still, I sat on the window ledge, crying until my throat became an aching lump. The professionals and Joyce waited. Joyce tried to reason with me. That just made me more upset.

I don't know how long I was on the window ledge for but eventually, I got down. In tiredness and despair,

I went downstairs with those adults, giving in to my fate.

I can't remember saying goodbye to Joyce. I just cried.

The professionals ushered me outside and into the back of their car. The man with dreadlocks took my luggage, as my little shrunken shoulders collapsed into the vehicle.

Joyce came outside to see me off. I gave her one last look; one last desperate attempt to connect with her. She had now taken off her glasses. Her eyes watered. This was the closest I'd ever seen her to tears. She said nothing, just looked at me.

Then the car drove off and I knelt up in the rear seat to view Joyce through the back window. As the distance between us grew, I watched her get smaller and smaller until, finally, she disappeared out of sight.

3

INSTITUTIONALISED

I was inconsolable in the car.

The man with dreadlocks gently tried to calm me down. He introduced himself as Kirk.

Was he my new foster parent?

But my mind didn't really have room to grapple with questions about where I was going. I was forced to deal with the rarest of griefs – being split from the foster carer I thought I'd spend the rest of my childhood with.

As we drove down south London's famous Walworth Road, I took in the final scenes of my hometown. These were scenes I had always taken for granted. I passed my local barbershop. Would I see the barber again? Or the kids from the adventure playground? The familiar parts of my childhood were vanishing without a trace.

I had been brutally torn from my childhood community, and no one seemed to care about it. How was this meant to be 'good' for me? This was a decision I just couldn't get my head around.

At some point during the journey, Karen explained that I was moving to a children's home. The two others in the car apparently worked there. I had no idea what a children's home was. This was the first I'd heard of one – and I'd had no notice, no warning or heads-up.

As the journey wore on, the grief of being split from Joyce merged with a looming fear of where I was moving to. I was dislocated with no sense of safety or protection. It was hard to believe that I was a child in a so-called 'care' system. Being uprooted and torn away from the maternal figure I loved and then shunted to a new home, full of strangers – that didn't feel like care or love.

I was told that my new home was in Bermondsey, another part of south-east London. Although a short drive away from Joyce's, the distance felt colossal.

Soon enough, we arrived at a sandy-brick house opposite a council estate. This was it. Roseberry Street Children's Home. My new home. My new Joyce.

The dread I was feeling bubbled up further as we parked up outside the house. Who was inside there? What sort of life awaited me on the other side of that door?

As we got out of the car, Karen left me in the hands of the care home workers and after a swift goodbye, she went on her way. She had done her bit. For her, this was likely a matter of clocking in and out. She didn't seem to care about the cloud of rejection I lived under. This was, for her, simply another shift.

Several adults were involved in moving me around, but I don't think any of them grasped just how terrifying this process was for me. I felt completely isolated.

I was handed my bag and, following the two professionals, feeling defeated, I made my way inside. From my perspective as a child, looking up at its exterior as I walked inside, the house looked imposing and far too big to feel like a home.

As the front door opened, I heard children. We walked into a reception area. I felt exposed in such an open space. More adults – staff members – and about half a dozen boys who looked around my age waited to greet me.

I observed the small crowd looking at me, unaware of what to do or how to act. I was a deer in headlights. I managed a bewildered 'hello' and then Kirk took me upstairs to what would be my new bedroom.

The house was spacious and clinical. The passage-ways were painted in neutral colours. Fire-hazard signs and extinguishers were dotted around. I even spotted a pay phone. This place felt like a larger version of the waiting areas at GP clinics. Worlds away from Joyce's small, warm and cosy council home. How the heck was this meant to be a home when it felt more like council offices?

Walking up the stairs, I glanced down at the boys who were still in the passageway. They all clearly lived here. They were fidgeting and distracted, waiting to go back to whatever playful task they were doing. I could see that for them, this sort of 'welcome-the-new-boy moment' wasn't anything new. Unlike with Joyce, where at least I felt like a priority, here I was just another case checking in.

I was finally shown to my bedroom. I walked inside, completely worn out and defeated. The walls were a warm blue. There was a single bed and a cabinet. Simple. There were no signs of the previous boy who would have lived here. The room was plain and functional – purpose-built for the string of kids who'd move in and out.

Kirk left me there. The moment he closed the door behind him, I collapsed on to the bed and began to cry again.

Sunlight poured through the small bedroom window. I wondered what Joyce would have been doing in that moment. It couldn't have been more than an hour since I'd left her, but already, she felt like a lifetime away.

I was clueless about my new life. There was no manual for being looked after; no user's guide on how to begin a new life in a children's home. I didn't know the word for it back then, but I felt abandoned. My biological parents didn't want me. Neither did Joyce. Nobody did, really. I figured I was an inconvenience for the adults I met, and when I became *too* inconvenient, they just moved me on. How long was I going to stay at this new place? How long until I was too old, too naughty or too unadoptable? Joyce had often told me she loved me. But do you send away the one you love into a care home?

I sat in my new bedroom, gripped by thoughts of Joyce and melancholy. I must have had some feelings of resentment towards her, but I would've gone back to her in a heartbeat.

At some point, Kirk came back to the bedroom to check on me.

'Ashley, you all right? Wanna give Joyce a quick call to tell her you're at your new home?' Kirk had a low, rough voice. But a caring one. He'd clearly grown up in London.

I speedily jumped off my new bed and made my way downstairs with Kirk. He took me to the home's office, full of files and paperwork, similar to the head teacher's office – the guy who had kicked me out of his primary school. Funny how a few documents can stand as the only record of a care kid's life sometimes.

I quickly found the phone and dialled Joyce's number. I knew it off by heart. Her phone rang. I stood there, desperate to hear her voice.

'Hello?' she said.

I was silent. I could feel my heart begin to race.

'Ashley?'

Her warm, Jamaican tone was too much. Again, tears began to flow. I tried to hold it all in as I heaved and spluttered down the phone. As well as Kirk, there were other adults in the office. Workers I knew absolutely nothing about. Yet here they were, observing me in all my vulnerability as I grieved. Because this *was* a type of bereavement. Although in this case, Joyce was just a short drive away.

As she spoke, her voice triggered a swell of despair inside of me. I could see her in my mind's eye, sat on her leather sofa in her headscarf. I could almost smell the scent of her seasoned chicken, knowing she'd soon begin to busy herself getting things ready for when the family would visit in the evening. But there I was in a children's home; a dingy office, surrounded by a host of strangers.

I eventually managed to mutter something into the phone.

I can't recall all Joyce's words, but I remember her saying that the move was for my own good. Really? That was the sum total of her explanation for kicking me out? Even today, as a grown man, I don't really understand what she meant. She added that she hoped to be able to see me soon. I didn't know what to believe.

Then the call ended. I stood there, phone in hand, not wanting to let it go, until Kirk ushered me out of the office.

Over the following days, I got to know more about Roseberry Street. Around half a dozen or so workers were in the home daily. They didn't live there. They worked shift patterns and so the staff would rotate day after day. That meant one day, Kirk would wake me up and then another person the day after. A batch of workers would clock in to supervise us boys for the day, and then another member of staff would take over for the night shift. By the time we woke up, they'd be out the door. This wasn't even close to the sense of family and consistency I'd felt at Joyce's.

How could I ever trust or connect with these people? This place was more like a run-down hotel than a home. Still, in time, I got to know the other boys – there was Dre, Aidan, Nathan, Phillip, Ola and others. Like me, they were all unwanted; all with their own stories of being let down and ending up in this place. Over time, some left and new boys came in. This house was a revolving door of workers and abandoned boys.

Most evenings the workers and boys would huddle in the living room to watch telly. 'You all right?' asked

Dre, as I eventually plucked up the courage to go in there.

I could tell Dre was a leader among the boys. Dark-skinned, tall and skinny, he had a natural ability at football and had been at the home the longest of every-one. It was almost baffling to observe how at ease he was there.

'I've been here for years now,' he told me. 'Don't worry, man, you'll get used to it.'

Alongside the living room, the house had a dining room and a few other spaces for computer games and recreational stuff. Outside was a spacious garden, where over time, I'd begin to play football with the other boys and get up to mischief.

Over the days, weeks and months I did get used to this new life. Being in care makes you a chameleon: you have to shift your exterior to fit in – something I would master. So although it could never be called a home, or a family, it was a place for us misfits. A care home for unwanteds; something we boys all had in common. And while the wound of leaving Joyce's cut deep, I was slowly able to allow myself to settle in.

Like myself, most of the boys in the house didn't go to school. Whether it was due to exclusion or straight-up truanting, they all had their reasons. And no one pushed them. With the consistent switching of workers, no one really seemed to be in charge or have a grasp on the day-to-day lives of the boys.

During those first weeks at the home, school days were filled with computer games, general mischief and banter. The staff would often take us on trips – to the local leisure centre swimming pool, park walks, bowling. My idea of family and home was what I knew of life at Joyce's. This didn't feel like that – this was more like a youth camp.

Undeniably, though, we had fun, until our uncapped recreational time occasionally descended into chaos. Often a fight or a tantrum would break out and that's when the care home staff would resort to restraining us.

On one occasion, Phillip kicked off over something. It must've been trivial because I can't remember what it was, but he began to throw stuff about. That's when a male member of staff forcibly threw him on the ground just at the top of the stairs and pinned him down, locking his arms behind his back.

There on the ground, I remember that Phillip's eyes were red, welling up, as his boyish bravado fought to hold back the tears. His face turned bright red, too, his young frame bearing the weight of being held down by a fully grown man. Did Phillip even know the name of that worker? Did he trust him? Or know him – even a little bit? All that aside, the man was massive. Phillip was a kid – maybe eight years old. Seeing him, a child, being handled like that unsettled me. Those moments felt more like custody than care.

While at Roseberry, I was restrained on several occasions myself – once for getting in a petty fight with one of the other boys. More than the physical harm that could come from these rebukes, it was the deep shame of being manhandled in your own 'home' by those who were supposed to love you that stung the most. The workers told us that restraints were a last resort when our behaviour got out of control. Joyce had never restrained me, but maybe, here in this new home, it *was* the only way, although many times I wondered if there was an alternative.

When it came to staff in the home, there were never any little family touches – things like hugs or kisses. But as a little boy in a new home, how do you summon up the courage to ask for a hug? I just accepted it. Maybe the restraints were a type of tough love.

While I often enjoyed my time with the boys, the dynamics of that house – the office, the restraints, the shifting workers – all conveyed the sense of being an inmate, rather than a cherished son. But maybe I didn't deserve to be a son.

So we boys didn't really bond with the staff – although I did grow to respect Kirk. And there was one other worker called Myles who was completely different to all the rest.

Myles was dark-skinned with plaits. Like Joyce, he was of Caribbean heritage, and when he spoke, his Grenadian dialect almost sounded like singing. He carried joy in his demeanour, which didn't always translate well with a bunch of care home boys. But that zeal, I'd say, is what set him apart.

4

COULD I FIT IN?

One particular afternoon, as I was sat playing the Play-station with Dre, Myles was on shift. He stood outside the door of the room we were in, peering at me thought-fully. Then he summoned me out to the hallway. Was I in trouble?

Myles paused and looked down in reflection. He then lifted his head, with his eyes centred on me. 'Do you want to go back to school?' he asked.

I didn't have to think hard about that one. What a ridiculous question. Nope! It was now months since I'd left Joyce's and even longer since I'd got kicked out of school. I'd got used to dossing. Furthermore, as school didn't seem to be important to the other boys in the home, why should I care? I had already missed a large chunk of the academic year. It wasn't worth getting back into that rut. If anything, going to school would set me apart from the other boys at Roseberry Street. And I'd had enough of being the odd one out. Here, I was at peace to just drift and be like the other boys I lived with.

'Ashley, I want us to get you into a new school,' Myles said kindly, but firmly. 'It's time that we got you back into learning.' I could see he was ready to argue on this one. And clearly, he had already determined that he was going to try and find a school for me.

In due course, Myles set up a meeting with the head teacher of the local Turringdon Primary School. I would've been nine years old. Even though the academic year was under way, Myles explained that the school was apparently open to finding out more about me.

Turringdon was a state school, just off the Old Kent Road. It was a grey day when we finally visited. On arrival, we were ushered to the head teacher's office. Myles strode in, head up, with his upbeat tone. I slumped behind, thinking back to my old school and the expulsion. This was a new school, though, a new opportunity, as Myles had reassured me.

On meeting the head teacher, Myles did most of the talking. I froze. Another tall, imposing man I didn't trust. Myles did his utmost to big me up: 'Ever since Ashley moved to Roseberry Street, he has lit up the home. He's so good with the other boys.'

He clearly couldn't have been talking about me. Would it work? I wondered. For all the adults I'd had to submit my life to in the care system, I didn't do well at meeting new ones. I couldn't shake the deep distrust and resentment I often felt towards them and I just felt uncomfortable around this head teacher.

A lot of grown-up talk took place between Myles and the head. And regardless of how I felt, I behaved well. I tried to be pleasant. I forced a lot of smiles. Surely, a good result?

After the meeting, Myles and I walked back to Rose-berry Street. Then, having dropped me off, he soon finished his shift and made his way home.

I often wondered what sort of home Myles (and the other staff) went back to after a shift. Did he live locally? Did he have a family? Maybe he lived across the road on the council estate and secretly checked in on us boys while we were sleeping. Or maybe he didn't. Maybe he just forgot about me once he got back to his own home and family. After all, as much as he was trying to help me find a school, he was getting paid for this task. His efforts weren't rooted in genuine care, I told myself. He was just good at his job.

We didn't have to wait too long for a response from Turringdon after our meeting. They refused me a place. Maybe I hadn't impressed the head during the meeting. Maybe the boys from Roseberry Street had a bad name among the teachers at Turringdon – that wouldn't have surprised me. Care home kids normally have bad repu-tations in their communities; there was always a stigma when it came to them. Even as a child, I was aware of it. But whatever the reason why they didn't want me, as usual, I wasn't told what it was.

If anything, I was relieved. But I can still recall Myles's disappointment when he broke the news to me. I wouldn't let myself believe that he cared, but it did make me curious all the same. Why did my school attendance appear to be so important to Myles? What-ever the reason, one thing was undeniable. I hated him for it.

Not long after Turringdon, Myles took me to visit another school just around the corner from Roseberry Street. Galleywall Primary.

On that occasion I didn't meet the head. Instead, I met the woman who would potentially become my teacher. Her name was Halle. She was Black, with a strong East End accent and thick dreadlocks. She had the same warmth as Mrs Oke, the teacher from my old primary school. And, just like Mrs Oke, Halle's classroom had the same colourful displays of animals, artwork, literature. There was a nostalgia and warmth about it all. Maybe there was a part of me that wanted to go back to school, after all.

Unlike the head at Turringdon, Halle spent most of her time talking to me, not Myles. And as reluctant as I was to open up, I soon found myself sharing about my life at Roseberry Street.

'What do you like about your home?' she asked.

'The boys are fun, and we go on lots of trips,' I told her shyly.

She then got me to read a book for a reading assessment and soon after that, Myles and I went back to Roseberry. Nothing major.

Not long after the meeting, Galleywall got in touch. To Myles's delight, the school, and Halle, invited me to permanently join them.

'Ashley. This is brilliant news. Congrats young man. Your life has changed for the better,' beamed Myles.

I was fairly impassive about the whole thing; I couldn't understand the significance of school. But Myles was thrilled.

It would've been during the spring of 1999 when I started at Galleywall. On the first morning, at 7am, Myles stormed into my room uninvited.

'Ashley, it's time for school. Up!' he barked. There was a ferocity in him that morning that rarely reared its head. 'Do you want to be late on your first day?'

I eventually made my way to the bathroom. It felt like Myles was following me around the house. From the bed-room to the bathroom to the kitchen downstairs. He was there loitering. Waiting for me. It was bloody annoying. Normally the workers 'supervised' us from a distance. Today, Myles was abnormally up close and focused on my every move. Had I brushed my teeth? Decent breakfast? Clean underwear? Workers didn't tend to pay so much attention to these details of our lives. This smelled of Joyce.

Once I was ready, Myles walked me to school. Until that point, only Joyce had ever done this. Although the school was just a stone's throw from Roseberry, that morning the walk felt excruciatingly long. But Myles soon eased up on the militant string of demands. His tone softened back to normal.

'How are you feeling?' he asked.

'Yeah, all right.'

I didn't give much away, although deep down, I was bricking it. The last time I'd gone to a school, I was handed an exclusion. I struggled to fit in with the other kids back then and I didn't trust the adults. Why would Galleywall be any different?

Strings of others were also making their way to school. Outside the school gate, parents were parting with their children, uttering goodbyes with affectionate hugs and kisses. Looking on, I felt a sadness and underlying jealousy. Why didn't I have a loving parent to give me a hug or kiss goodbye?

I muttered a curt 'see you later' to Myles and briskly walked through the gate, school bag in hand, to begin my first day. I didn't want an awkward goodbye and I didn't want Myles to be weird. We never hugged. That wasn't our thing at Roseberry. No use forcing it now.

In that moment, walking through the school gate didn't feel too significant. The grey concrete of the school playground with yellow lines to mark out the makeshift footy pitch, the Victorian red-brick school building, and the morning frenzy of kids running around blissfully before the start of the school day – it all felt familiar. It felt like Falondale Primary.

Before long, the school bell rang, and a teaching assistant ushered me to my classroom. As I filed through with the other students to class, the nerves resurfaced.

I walked into the colourful classroom, not particularly mindful of the other students. And there was Halle, stood in front of the blackboard. Sunshiny.

She had a seat prepared for me at a table and after we'd all settled down, she introduced me to the class. Halle had an undeniable authority and commanded instant respect; but there was also a deep warmth. I don't know what it was, but she was one of the few adults I felt safe around.

'Ashley's starting with us today. Please do make him feel welcome.'

She then proceeded to walk around the room, handing out exercise books. As she came my way to hand me a notepad, she gently rested a hand on my shoulder in passing and then moved on. I felt warm and fuzzy inside.

For many of our lessons I was sat next to a boy named Kaseem. Chubby and bookish, he took every task seriously. Weirdly, his focus on being the best at every subject and finishing first sparked a competitive edge within me. This was a dynamic I'd never had at school before. Over time, we became friends. And while I still had my spells of distraction and playing up, Halle had a calming effect on my temperament. This class was the closest I'd come to feeling accepted since life at Joyce's. Looking back, I think Halle had a hand in that. She just had a gift for making us all feel included. No one was better than anyone else in her estimation. And, perhaps because of Halle, the outbursts I'd had at Falondale Primary were nowhere near as prevalent these days.

I remember after one particular English lesson, Halle came over to me and commented on how well I was doing. She smiled, her eyes warmly gazing at me. Despite how disarming she was, however, I knew well enough not to fully buy into her words. Always leave room for doubt, I reminded myself. As the situation with Joyce had demonstrated, I always had to be ready for rejection – to be let down. I needed a cold heart to handle being a child in care. But still, at the very least, it was nice to hear those words.

In the first few days and weeks of starting at Galleywall, Myles, without fail, would make sure I was up promptly at seven in the morning, ready for school. If he was on shift, it would mean an intrusive knock on the bedroom door. If he was at his own home, he'd call up the office to make sure someone was on my case. And the more persistent he became in this pursuit, the more irritating he grew.

So determined was Myles to pursue his school campaign, however, that over time, school became a normal habit. Leaving the boys at Roseberry Street as they slept or were just gingerly crawling out of bed, I'd walk to school with whichever worker was on shift, anticipating the day ahead. And sometimes, I even enjoyed those morning walks.

Although having been excluded from Falondale othered me, and that feeling of rejection made me believe I was unable to flex with the other 'normal' kids, in time, at Galleywall, I began to believe I could fit in. For the hours I was there, I felt as normal as I possibly could. Entering the school gates, I'd rush to meet my mate Jack who lived near Roseberry and was in the same year as me. We'd run to the marked-out concrete football pitch for a kickabout.

For all the boyhood resentment I held for Myles in his persistence in forcing me back to school, perhaps part of me was secretly grateful. But I never admitted that to him. And arriving back at Roseberry each day, there'd always be the odd joke or two from one of the other boys. 'Allow, school man – stop being a neek,' was a common remark. So as much as I warmed to school, I'd never admit my affection for it in front of the other boys.

School life soon began to pour into my weekends, when I'd hang out with classmates Kaseem and Jack. Against the backdrop of the local estate and an unloved high street, we reverted to playing knock down ginger and chilling at Jack's house.

On one particular Saturday afternoon, we were in Jack's front garden. I needed the loo, and so he signalled me inside. I walked in, through a narrow passageway. Jack's home felt cosy. It was decorated with family photos. Roseberry Street didn't have photos on the walls. It felt weird being in a 'normal' home again.

Not entirely sure as to where the bathroom was, I took a right turn into the living room, only to see Jack's parents cuddled up on the sofa watching telly. Normal enough. But in that moment, a flush of embarrassment sparked inside. I gave a curt, bashful greeting and quickly left the room.

Seeing Jack's parents together in Saturday normalcy sparked a surge of emotion in me. That quick, fleeting glance hurt me. Where were *my* parents? *My* family? Just being in a mate's house alerted me to all that I lacked and reminded me of the family I didn't have. This could well have been the first time I saw two parents and lovers, up close, enjoying each other's company in the comfort of their own home. This wasn't a model I was used to. It was unsettling. *My* normal was shift workers and boys moving in and out of that big, cold house.

I eventually found the bathroom and locked myself inside, gazing into nothing. I knew Jack didn't real-ise how fortunate he was to have a secure home and parents. I envied him. Not because he was the funniest, the smartest or because he had the best trainers in class. But because he had a home. But then I put on my bravado, threw on a smile and got back to Jack and Kaseem.

At some point during my time at Roseberry Street, Karen, the social worker, came to visit me with a man I had never met before. Taking a seat, Karen gave me that look. The one of supposed concern, that was really an act. At least that's how I saw it.

'How's it going here?' she asked.

'Yeah, cool,' I muttered back.

We sat there. Moments passed in silence.

'It's great that you're going to school,' she said. Her tone lifted, desperately trying to steer the awkwardness of our chat to somewhere more upbeat.

Karen had barely visited since taking me away from Joyce. Maybe seeing me now reminded her of her guilt; her complicity in ruining my life. Social workers were meant to help, but she had done the opposite for me.

I didn't give her much. She wasn't to be relied on. The ease with which Karen was able to uproot me from life at Joyce's showed me just how stone cold she was. The smiles and that gentle tone were not to be trusted. She continued to look at me with an unwavering intensity. Then, eventually, she gestured to the man sitting next to her.

'This is Mr Patel,' she said.

An older, plump man of Asian heritage, Mr Patel sat there smiling at me, peering through glasses with a face full of facial hair.

'We have decided he'll be your new social worker.'

Karen leaned in, looking at me. 'Ashley, it's time for me to move on,' she said.

I sat there looking between Mr Patel and Karen. I didn't feel an ounce of emotion at the news. Completely indifferent. I wouldn't miss Karen. She didn't even come close to Joyce. Maybe I was still numb after Joyce or maybe Karen simply didn't mean much to me. But one thing was for sure: having experienced the rejection of Joyce, I was able to stomach others leaving my life. I had been primed and prepared for abandonment ever since Joyce let me go.

After some further pleasantries, the two of them left. Mr Patel said he'd be visiting soon. And I never saw Karen again.

5

THE ANGEL

Mr Patel always carried a briefcase and seemed nice enough. While he showed an interest in how I was doing, he seemed far more preoccupied with preparing me for my future, regardless of my current circumstances. In that sense, he was very different from Karen.

Without Karen, he had a greater air of authority, too. He sat next to me and Myles on the living room sofa. He took out a form.

'School?' Tick.

'Is Ashley visiting the doctor's regularly?'

'Of course,' said Myles.

Tick.

'Ashley, how do you feel in this home? Are you happy with this arrangement?'

I looked down. 'Yeah, it's all right,' I replied.

Did he actually expect honesty from me? To hear that on occasion I had a laugh with the other boys, but deep down, all I wanted was to go back to Joyce's? But what the heck would that achieve?

After a slight pause, Mr Patel ticked another box.

I hated social worker assessments. It felt to me like Mr Patel didn't really care and he certainly didn't have the power to change anything. Honesty was no use with these people. It seemed to me that as long as Mr Patel ticked boxes on pieces of paper, he would convince his social work bosses that I was okay and prove to them that he was doing a good job. Even if he meant well, I knew better than to trust people like him – the professionals – whatever the guise.

Once he'd completed his form, Mr Patel slipped it into his briefcase, but then moved on to another issue. He leaned in closer to look at me, his bushy eyebrows merging as he peered down at me through his glasses. I looked around sheepishly. I felt awkward.

'Ashley, I would like to talk to you about your mother. What do you know about her?'

His words stopped me in my tracks. There was something really unsettling about having a man I barely knew ask me such personal questions. The photo I'd received when I was at Joyce's and the anecdotes she'd told me were the small fragments I had of my mum. They weren't a lot, but they were precious, and I didn't want to share them with this stranger.

'I had a photo of her once . . . she's blonde,' I stuttered.

He didn't press me on the photo. Instead, he asked, 'Did Joyce or Karen ever tell you stuff about her?'

'Karen told me some stuff. Her life was hard and all that,' I said. But I wasn't prepared to reveal what Joyce had shared; I wouldn't open up about the bag of presents she'd sent to me that Christmas or the fact that on a few occasions my mum had visited Joyce in the dark of night when I was asleep. I understood enough to know that Joyce would've got in trouble if Mr Patel had found that out.

He paused and continued to look at me intently. 'Ashley, I have something to tell you about your mother.'

I looked on. Waiting.

'I have been in touch with her, Ashley. She wants to meet you.'

All I could think about was the image of the blonde lady in the photo Joyce had given me all those years ago. Ever since I lost it in the school playground, I'd wondered what she was like. If I'd ever meet her. My mind raced. In my head, she was an angel. Pure. Innocent. In my boyish thinking, I never really made the connection between her and my reality of being shunted into this system. I never had her down as a potential cause for why I was looked after. I never blamed her.

But then, I'd never had to deal with the prospect of meeting her.

Mr Patel's voice soon interrupted the growing whirl of thoughts. 'So, Ashley. Would you like to meet your mother?'

I nodded instantly. 'Yes, please,' I said politely, as if seeking permission to go to the toilet at school.

It was all a blur from there. Mr Patel left at some point, but I sat there, transfixed in thought, wondering what my mum might be like. Maybe she would take me away from Roseberry Street. Was this a chance to be normal, to have a family? I wondered if she'd look the same as she had in the photo. Did she live near Roseberry Street? Somewhere in Bermondsey? Maybe I'd even passed her on a local street without knowing.

Any time I saw a blonde woman after that meeting with Mr Patel, my mind soared with wild curiosity about this woman who had given birth to me. Would she like me? Did she love me?

Mr Patel set in motion the arrangements for me to meet my mum. And while I was curious, scared, anxious and even excited, I never told any of the other boys in the house about her. I already knew that some of them wouldn't get such an opportunity to meet a parent or family member. These boys didn't have relatives queuing up to see them. Even as a boy, I understood that my news about my mum would be too triggering for a lot of them.

And for once, I felt a little bit fortunate. Still, over the days and weeks that followed, I forgot about the meeting with Mr Patel and got back into regular life at Roseberry. I was still going to school and generally getting up to light mischief with the other boys during the evenings. That was until the day finally came.

Just like the day I left Joyce's, it was sunny. I was told my mum was due to arrive at Roseberry Street around midday. One of the workers had taken the boys out in the morning, giving me the space to meet my mum. Just as I had on my first day at Roseberry Street, I sat in my bedroom, staring at the warm blue walls.

What would my mother's voice sound like? How tall was she? Would she hug me? Where had she been all this time? I had no answers . . . just endless questions.

Myles didn't tend to work on Saturdays, but on this occasion, he was there. There was a warmth in seeing him turn up that morning. He insisted that I try to appear tidy. That was a detail and consideration the other workers wouldn't have noticed or cared about.

'Ashley, do you want me to iron a shirt for you?' he asked.

'Okay, thanks.'

I watched Myles iron my shirt. And despite the burning questions and deep anxiety I felt, I didn't say anything. I had to keep it together and be strong.

I didn't know what to expect of the woman who was my mum. Maybe she'd decide, after meeting me, that she never wanted to see me again. Would this be another instance of rejection for me?

The waiting was unbearable. The silence too loud. There was nothing I could do apart from wander around the house, plagued with thoughts about what was about to happen. I eventually ended up in the kitchen.

A knock at the door, then silence. Myles went to answer. I held my breath.

'Mr Patel, come in!'

A sigh of relief.

Myles walked over to me with Mr Patel alongside him. 'Hello, Ashley. How are you feeling?' asked Mr Patel.

'I'm okay, thanks,' I said with a feigned smile.

The remaining workers who were still in the house also came into the kitchen. It was now nearly midday. The adults milled around the room. There were some light refreshments – some unappetising tuna sandwiches cut into triangles with juice and sliced fruit. I sat by the corner of the kitchen table.

I assumed this was what an awkward family gathering felt like – the type talked about by mates at school. Mr Patel held a plastic cup in one hand and a sandwich in the other as he whispered intently into Myles's ear.

I felt extremely alone, internally leaping between sheer excitement and fear. Sweat dripped down beneath my pressed shirt. My palms were sweaty. I had a neat low trim following a recent visit to the barber.

Some of the workers asked me how I was feeling. I responded with pleasantries. How could any of these adults expect me to open up about how I was really feeling? And I was fairly sure they didn't care either way. It was enough of a moment to be meeting my mum, but to do it in a kitchen full of professionals all looking on? Maybe I should've asked Myles or Mr Patel if the other adults could leave. But since when did adults care about or listen to what I wanted?

Through the chatter and low buzz, there came another knock at the door. Silence ensued immediately. Both Myles and Mr Patel left the kitchen and made their way to the front door.

As if by a silent command, myself and all the workers lined the back kitchen wall with our eyes fixed on the door. It wasn't that long ago that I had arrived at Roseberry and been shown into that clinical passageway myself. I wondered how my mum found it walking into the house for the first time.

Myles and Mr Patel slowly re-entered the kitchen, looking at me sensitively. Behind them, two women. Not one but two. Two pretty blonde women at that. They stood at the kitchen door, waiting to be invited in.

Mr Patel walked over to me.

I looked at the women. One was smiling, but also whimpering in an attempt to control the flow of her tears and breathing. Her face red. The other lady put an arm on her back.

I looked up at them. I squinted, trying to remind myself of the photo Joyce had given me and to envisage what my mum looked like. Which of these two women most resembled the person in the photo?

'Ashley, want to guess which one is your mum?' Mr Patel chimed in.

I smiled nervously.

Really? I had to choose? Mr Patel's voice brought me back to the reality that there was a group of people in the room watching my every move. Watching the women. The first time I was meeting my mum since being put into care, and I was being observed by a bunch of care-home workers.

I had a gut instinct about which one was my mum, but I was reluctant to play guess who. I didn't want to get it wrong. The stakes felt too high. Still, I pointed at the lady crying.

Through her tears, she smiled and slowly nodded.

And without prompting, I ran towards her. She knelt down, with open arms, and I jumped into her embrace. She was soft and smelled of sweet perfume. As we hugged each other, I could feel her blonde hair brush the top of my head. She was breathing heavily. I was crying silent tears. I hid myself in her arms. Blocking out the onlookers. The professionals.

By this point my mum was inconsolable. 'I love you, my son. I'm so sorry.'

I didn't say anything. I just stayed wrapped in her arms. Secure for as long as she would allow.

For a moment, there was peace. Warmth. A rare hug. This is what I've been missing, I thought. This is what I've wanted all along.

Fleetingly, the Roseberry Street kitchen morphed into the warm home I'd always dreamed of. Sunlight pierced through the kitchen windows, lighting the magnolia walls. Afternoon bliss.

My mum eventually stood up.

'This is my friend Tanya,' she said referencing the blonde lady beside her.

'I'm so happy to finally meet you, Ashley,' Tanya said, now wiping tears from her own cheeks.

It was weird seeing Tanya, a stranger, overwhelmed with emotion about meeting me. I wasn't used to the affection I was being showered with.

Even though I'd just met my mum, there was an instant, unspoken bond. Everyone looked on until, finally, Myles took me, my mum, Mr Patel and Tanya to another room. Sitting in a more intimate space, I had no idea what to say. For all my questions, all I could do was look at my mum. Likewise, she looked back at me. She made a point of apologising a lot.

Mr Patel interjected. 'Ashley, I have agreed with your mum that we can explore the possibility of her visiting a few times a year. Maybe next time she can take you somewhere local for lunch?'

I nodded, my eyes still fixed on Mum. The next visit felt like far too much to comprehend. I was still grasping the fact that my mum was in the same room as me now. Right in front of me. That I had touched and smelled her.

On Mr Patel's prompt, the time eventually arrived for my mum to leave. We hugged some more and reluctantly parted ways. And as short as that first meeting had been, I knew my life would never be the same.

The rest of that day was a blur. The boys eventually came back home, but there was only one thing for me to think about . . . Mum. Maybe someone did love me, after all. And maybe I could have a future with my mum, away from the care system.

For all my distrust of social workers, I was grateful that Mr Patel had arranged for me to meet my mum. I relived that short encounter frequently – on the school playground with classmates, alone in my bedroom. Normally, boys of my age got excited for birthday presents, holidays, the chance to see their football team play. For me, it was all about meeting my mum.

6

CARRY THE LOAD

Not long after that first meeting I saw my mum again.

Away from the glare of the multitude of professional onlookers and as close to private as it could be for a child residing in a care home, this was, perhaps, the first proper meeting.

Mr Patel allowed us to meet for thirty minutes or so at a local restaurant called the Wimpy. It was near Joyce's. As he walked me there, through the hustle and bustle of Walworth Road, he explained that this was a chance for me to get to know my mum a bit more and that he would supervise us from a distance.

When she'd visited me at Roseberry Street, I'd been waiting for her. This time, she was the one waiting for me. As I walked into the Wimpy, she was sat at a table, nervously looking around. She was still as pretty as I remembered her to be in that photo Joyce had given me. Maybe she looked a bit older but the newness of seeing her hadn't worn off – it was still hard to believe that, after all this time, I was actually seeing my mum in the flesh. I was as nervous as I was thrilled.

Her blonde hair stood out against the dreary backdrop of the burger diner. I imagined a halo on top of her head. Could she be the angel who would one day take me away from my care-kid reality?

Mr Patel gestured me to sit with her. Then he took a seat a few rows away from us but still within earshot of our conversation. Why was Mr Patel policing this intimate moment with my mum? I wondered. Didn't he trust me? Maybe he thought I'd say something bad about the care I was receiving at Roseberry.

My mum was looking at me. Teary-eyed again. She didn't say much at the start.

I knew her name was Christie and that she'd had me as a teenager. I had gleaned that much from the records and life story documents. However, the files and drip feed of information from social workers didn't compare one bit to the reality of sitting right in front of her. Gazing at her. Close up.

An intimate glance into her eyes told me more about who she was than any file, social worker report or life story document could. I could tell that she was kind. A decent person. I could tell that she cared about me, maybe even loved me. Could I also sense a sadness? Maybe it was to do with her life; or maybe it was to do with me . . .

When I lived with Joyce, she would often remark on how my hair would turn a blondish brown in the sun. Seeing my mum, I could now tell that I got that from her. And looking into my mum's eyes I searched for my own reflection. I needed a hint of who I was, who I belonged to. I needed a sign that I wasn't a mistake.

Everything that happened during that meeting was significant. I ordered some sort of burger and chips. She bought it. I marked it as the first time she'd ever bought me lunch. Things that the kids at school took for granted with their families were great milestones for me.

Her attempts to keep the conversation light and fun inevitably ended up somewhere more painful for her. It's easy to understand now the guilt she might have felt back then for me being taken into care. I can't remember everything about that conversation, but my mum ended almost every sentence with an apology.

'Ashley, I know you must have a lot of questions about me, your dad and why you're in care. But I am so sorry that I wasn't able to . . .' A deep cry erupted from within her before she could finish.

I had a lot of questions, but I didn't know how to ask them. I looked at her, reading into her every word, look and action – trying to make up for lost time. All I knew was that what seemed to be her sadness made me sad.

'How's the children's home?' she asked.

'It's fine, thanks. I told the boys I would meet you today,' I replied.

'Joyce talked about you a lot, too,' I said.

'I love Joyce,' my mum replied. 'She promised me she'd always tell you who I was. Joyce said she'd make sure you remembered me . . .' And, once again, a rush of tears flowed down my mum's cheeks as she spoke about Joyce.

I found comfort in knowing that we both had a love for Joyce. Common ground. But there were too many questions for this soon-to-end Wimpy session. I didn't know what to say. For now, I was just content with the warm, fuzzy feeling I felt in my tummy just being around my mum.

Sure enough, Mr Patel soon sauntered over to our table. 'Ashley, can you say bye to your mum? It's time to go now.'

We hugged and I walked off with Mr Patel. My mum sat there, watching us leave. As I neared the door, I looked back to glimpse her one more time.

I didn't know if I would see her again.

Mr Patel had met my mum a few times. I'd later find out that he'd had to assess whether she was in a fit state to be reintroduced back into my life. With social services, she was on trial. But in my mind, she could do no wrong. Over the following months, we would meet a few more times, until Mr Patel decided regular visits could be a permanent fixture in my life.

Eighteen months or so into life at Roseberry Street, things were going well. Meeting my mum had sparked a new optimism in me. I'd run around the school playground boasting about knowing her. Back when I lived with Joyce, I had brandished that photo of my mum as proof of my family. Now, however, I could say that I met her regularly at the Wimpy.

I had friends at school and hadn't been suspended. Myles had become someone who I'd grown to like, maybe even trust. But most significantly, I was getting to know my mum. By my lowly standards, life was good.

Then, just when I felt like I had a reason for hope, Myles had another life update for me.

One day, as I was playing with the other boys, he interrupted our fun, taking me to the kitchen for another one of his chats. He had that look. Serious. He had something important to tell me.

'Ashley, I know when you moved to live at Roseberry Street, you really didn't want to be here.'

I had no idea where he was going with this.

'Well, a home like Roseberry Street is never meant to be a permanent placement or a forever home. It's a temporary arrangement until we can find boys like you a long-term family to live with,' he said, seeming to tread carefully with his words, examining my facial reactions to gauge how I felt about what he was saying.

My heart sank.

He continued. 'Ashley, Mr Patel has found a woman who is interested in fostering you.'

I stared blankly at Myles. The thought of living with another stranger was too overwhelming for me. This was heavy.

He paused, but I could see he was genuinely pleased at this turn of events. He went on to reassure me this was for the best. For me, it seemed anything but.

Myles and Mr Patel had arranged that I'd live with this potential foster mum for a couple of weeks as a taster to see whether she'd want to take me in for the long haul.

'Ashley, this is your chance to be part of a normal foster family. All you need to do is show her just how lovely and nice you are. Then she'll foster you permanently,' Myles said.

I was being put on trial by professionals. It rested on me to prove to yet another stranger how lovable and compliant I could be. I had to show that I could function in a 'normal' family. Because, after all, it was up for debate. Could I prove that I wasn't dysfunctional and broken beyond the point of repair? Could I be a 'normal' kid inside a 'normal' family? Only if I passed this 'test' would the woman take me in.

The thought of leaving the boys at Roseberry Street was really upsetting. The energy required to settle into a new home, meet a new bunch of people and learn to be part of a new community all felt too much and I was dreading it. But as ever, I kept my thoughts and feelings to myself.

Soon, I was being driven to my temporary foster home. It was a Saturday and Myles was in the car.

'Ashley,' he began. 'The lady who will foster you for the next couple of weeks is called Carmen. She has two older sons – the younger one, a teenager, lives with her. They live in Nunhead, Peckham.'

'Okay,' I replied. I felt dismal. I don't think anyone around me, Myles included, truly understood the burden of having to go to another home and pretend to be the happy looked-after kid. Just like fading popstars, care kids have a shelf life. And soon enough, we will always be dropped by the ones who are meant to love us. Was

Myles now parring me off? Was he subtly passing me on? Shirking responsibility? Maybe he, like Joyce, had had enough of me.

We eventually parked up outside a semi-detached, red-brick house on a residential road.

'We're here,' said Myles.

We grabbed my sports bag from the boot and walked up to Carmen's house. Myles knocked on the front door.

I didn't know what I was expecting. A wave of nerves whirled inside me. I looked at the imposing front door, which seemed enormous to me, a small ten-year-old.

The door opened and we were greeted by a slim Black lady who could have been somewhere in her mid-forties. I looked up at her and said hello. She greeted Myles and me, ushering us inside.

It was warm, homely. Food seasoning and air freshener pierced my nostrils, as we walked through a narrow passageway and took a left into her living room.

'Ashley, just leave your bag outside, please,' Carmen said.

The living room had plush sofas – a two-seater and a single – positioned around a television. The walls were covered with a cream wallpaper which had a floral pattern. At the other end of the living room was a dining table, and a chunky grey PC was tucked in the corner on a cabinet.

It wasn't comparable to Joyce's but at least it didn't have the clinical air of Roseberry Street. After exchanging a few pleasantries with Carmen, Myles was quick to leave. 'Ashley, you'll be great. Speak soon,' he said to me, then he gave one last look of fondness and Carmen saw him out.

As the two of them left the living room, I sat down and took in my new surroundings, with no clue of what to do next.

It was nearing evening when Myles left. Carmen took me upstairs to show me my bedroom.

'Do you like chicken?' she asked.

'Yes,' I replied politely.

'Okay. Well, I'm just finishing off dinner. Take this for now,' she said, handing me a puzzle to complete as she swept off to the kitchen. A puzzle to immerse myself in this new home. No proper chat. No questions. No 'Are you okay?'

I felt like an imposter. Despite knowing next to nothing about Carmen, I now had to rely on her for food, shelter and care for the next couple of weeks. Yet as uncomfortable, and maybe even as sad as I felt, I knew I had to make it work. I had to be courteous and compliant enough for Carmen to want to have me around for longer. This was the audition of a lifetime. A chance to have a home. All I had to do was follow the rules, suppress any negative emotions or reactions and act happy. After all, it had been made clear to me that I had no other option – Roseberry Street would only take me up to my very early teenage years. And after that, I could end up anywhere. Another home? Part of a gang? In a hostel? So as much as I hated all these moves, I was somehow mindful of the fact that for looked-after children like me, things could often end up terrible. I was lucky. I knew that in reality, things could get much worse for me than Roseberry Street or this new lady, Carmen.

I never expected or even hoped for the perfect family. I just had to survive.

Before long, dinner was ready, and by then, I had made a start on the puzzle. As we ate at the dinner table, I thought with fondness about the chaos of the other boys and the hustle and bustle of a multitude of workers around me. Who would've thought I'd miss Roseberry so much! I wouldn't tell Carmen any of that, though. I'd only be grateful and pleasant.

We didn't talk much that evening. Carmen's son Reece was out. I was curious to meet and get to know him. I knew he was aged around fifteen or sixteen, and I worried about how we'd get on. After all, it was made clear to me that it was my job to get on with everyone if I was to stand a chance of Carmen taking me in permanently.

Finally, I was in bed where I lay awake, staring at the ceiling in the dark. At some point, I heard the opening and shutting of the front door. It must've been Reece. My test for acceptance would truly begin tomorrow.

7

CHILDHOOD AUDITION

It was a bright Sunday morning. Sunlight washed through the lace curtain of my new, temporary bedroom. The sinking feeling of being in an alien home hit me but I didn't have time to indulge it.

'Ashley, it's time to get up. We're going to church,' said Carmen, poking her head around the bedroom door.

I hadn't been to church since I left Joyce's and I had no interest in going back. But I knew I had to make this work. If church was part of the contract for acceptance, for a home, then so be it.

I didn't have many clothes, and I certainly didn't have anything formal. After a brief wash in what felt like a foreign bathroom, I threw on a T-shirt and jeans and made my way downstairs. Still no sign of Reece.

Carmen was cooking breakfast. 'Ashley, I go to a local church called the Salvation Army. There's a lot of young people. I think you'll enjoy it.' Carmen spoke in short, curt sentences. She commanded a respect that I'd never afforded the Roseberry staff, even if only because she stirred mild fear in me.

On my first full day at this new home, I'd have preferred to stay indoors and settle down. Church was the last thing on my mind. Yet, I understood enough about foster carers and social workers to know there was no point in saying how I really felt. As ever, I'd go along with the whims and decisions of an adult I barely knew.

After breakfast, Carmen went to put on her church clothes while I watched children's telly. Anxiety bubbled inside. Who would I meet at church? What would they think of me? I was done with meeting new people and settling into new spaces. I just wanted to be alone. But any time I felt sad, I reminded myself that this home was an opportunity and I had to make it work.

Sitting in the living room, I heard the click of heels as Carmen walked down the stairs. She came into the living room in a matching black blazer and skirt, with a white shirt underneath. The letter S was embroidered on the lapels of her blazer, adding a sense of militancy to her appearance. She wore a hat, also with an S plastered on the front. This was her church uniform. It looked militant and heightened my nerves even more.

I followed Carmen to her car, and we drove to the church. By this point in my life I was accustomed to being driven to unknown places by people I barely knew. But it didn't make this drive any more bearable. En route, she picked up an elderly lady called Josephine. I sat in the back of the car, silent, as they mused and chatted in the front.

We soon arrived at the local Salvation Army. Walking into the church foyer, I felt smaller and more isolated than ever. I was a child, stranded in a sea of unknown people.

Carmen greeted various congregants. They were predominantly white and all wearing that peculiar Salvation Army uniform. The kids were dressed in blue or red shirts which also sported a white S on the top left side.

Although we were in Peckham, a place of broad culture and diversity, this room felt a million miles from London. As Carmen moved across the church hall, making small talk with others, my small head darted around, taking in these new scenes.

There was a platform with a drum kit, piano and brass instruments. There was a podium. On the walls, religious paintings and Bible scriptures.

I wasn't introduced to many people. Instead, I was Carmen's silent guest. She gestured towards me to a few people, who smiled and muttered some platitudes. That made me feel even more uncomfortable. Maybe I was Carmen's charity case – the object of her 'Christian duty'. I got it into my head she was taking me in so that she could appear to be a good Christian for all these white religious people. She didn't genuinely care about me. Being in that church made my blood boil. I didn't want to be there, on show to all those strangers.

We sat down for the commencement of the service. Then, all of a sudden, a bunch of people walked on to the platform and took up the instruments. After a quick welcome, they began to play and lead the church in hymns. The booming sound of singing, accompanied by brass and percussion filled the room.

I felt out of place. Everyone else wore beaming smiles and was part of a family unit. They all seemed happy. But I felt like a stray, reluctantly scooped up by Carmen and made to endure a service with people I couldn't relate to. As much as I hated to admit it, I missed the boys at Roseberry Street; I missed Myles. Just as I'd been settling into my world at the children's home, I'd once again been shunted somewhere else.

After church we went back to Carmen's house. As she opened the front door, I could hear garage music blaring from inside, and when we walked in, Reece was in the hallway.

'Reece, this is Ashley,' Carmen said, gesturing towards me. I forced a smile.

'Wagwann, bruv,' Reece belted back, accompanied with a fist spud.

I instantly felt a level of comfort and normality in meeting him after the ordeal of the Salvation Army. Reece appeared to be effortlessly cool. He sported a Nike tracksuit and Air Force 1 trainers and had the sharpest trim. Aftershave pierced my nostrils as he made his way back upstairs to his bedroom.

'Reece!' Carmen shouted in his direction. 'You said you'd clean the car!'

Before I knew it, Carmen had enlisted me to help Reece with the task. As I followed him outside, scrubbing and rinsing his mum's Vauxhall Corsa, I couldn't help but wonder if I'd make a good brother for him. Did he really want another kid living in his house, sharing his mum? Foster care is never just about the foster carer – it needs to be a family decision; but in that moment, I didn't have the balls to ask him if he'd want someone like me to become his family. I just hoped that he could accept me. Still, trying to be accepted was tiring. I was just a kid. But even so, the thought of having a big brother, someone to look up to, did secretly appeal to me.

Over those couple of weeks at Carmen's, I can't recall having many chats with her. Maybe she was the silent type, I thought. She fed, clothed and took me to Galley-wall School diligently, but I can't say I got to know her much. But perhaps that was something I didn't have the luxury of hoping for. At that point, even a roof over my head for the long haul was an aspiration that at times felt too lofty.

As my time with Carmen and Reece came to an end, I was secretly hoping that she didn't want to take me in. And when Myles arrived to take me back to Roseberry Street I was relieved. After thanking Carmen courte-ously, I left in the hope that I'd never have to live with her again.

'How was it?' Myles asked with excitement as I got in the back of the car.

'I really liked it,' I lied.

'Fantastic. I knew you would,' Myles said enthusiasti-cally as we drove off.

Deep down I was thankful to be going back to Rose-berry, a place that now felt familiar, even if not like a family. At least there we didn't have to pretend we were a family. I didn't have to fight for the approval of workers. It was known there that we were rejects and dysfunctional. I didn't feel any pressure to be something I wasn't. I didn't have to fake a family.

I had a warm feeling seeing the other boys – Dre and Aidan especially, as we'd grown particularly close – and over the next few weeks, I settled back into life at Roseberry Street and school. I began to feel my regular self again, until, one day, Myles took me aside for another one of his chats.

'Ashley, there's been a bit of a development,' he said, giving me one of his intense looks.

I was desperately hoping it wasn't the news I was dreading. I began to breathe deeply.

'Carmen has offered to take you in as her foster child on a permanent basis!' Myles was beaming.

My belly sank. For a moment, I forgot where I was. I wanted to cry. I wanted to beg Myles profusely not to make me go there. As imperfect as it was, I wanted to stay at Roseberry Street. But despite all of that, I simply forced a smile. Once again, I had to make this work. I had to make myself settle into a new family setting. This wasn't about what was convenient. It was about survival.

That evening, over dinner, Myles told the boys. I knew I'd miss them, although we never showed any sense of hurt or vulnerability. Dre was older than me and we knew he'd have to leave soon, too. Where would he go? He didn't have any offers from foster carers. He'd probably have to go to a care home for older boys. I wondered if I would ever see him – or any of them – again? I wouldn't say we'd become brothers, but we had a fondness and respect for where we'd all come from. Life wasn't easy for us. The basics, like family and belonging, were foreign concepts, yet there was a connection and a comfort in knowing that we were all unwanted.

Despite how I felt, however – despite the growing fear of moving in with Carmen – leaving Joyce's had been enough of a lesson for me to know that protesting about these things didn't change anything. And this development was light work compared to leaving Joyce's.

I knew I had to have a thick skin. Crying or showing emotion wasn't going to help me. Nobody cared. I had grown numb to the reality of being shunted between homes. And as long as I could continue the visits with my mum, maybe I'd be okay. What's more, a niggling feeling of guilt had begun to bubble inside of me: the boys at Roseberry Street would've given anything to be considered for a foster family, yet here I was, unhappy at the prospect. I didn't realise how lucky I was, I told myself. I should count my blessings and take what many care home kids would consider to be the opportunity of a lifetime.

After Myles broke the news, I began to count down the moments before I'd inevitably leave Roseberry Street. The final days there were a blur. There was the last football match, the last day out, the last computer game, us boys fooling around in recreational bliss, forgetting about the reality of our lives.

But the regular day-to-day chaos continued. Because such was the culture of that home that me leaving wasn't a significant moment. Boys moved in and out of Roseberry on a regular basis. I was just another one.

However, I do remember one of my last moments with Myles.

'Ashley, I am so proud of you,' he said, and he hugged me. I'll never forget that. Perhaps he could see that I was despondent about moving to Carmen's because he looked me right in the eye with deep concern and said, 'Ashley – you have to make this new home work.'

I never saw Myles again for the rest of my life in care.

8

A FORCED FIT

Parting with Myles and the other boys was swift. And as quickly as I had left Carmen's, I was now back there. Only this time, permanently.

Mr Patel accompanied me. And he explained that I would continue to see my mum while living with Carmen – he was adamant about that, which was one good thing, I supposed.

A lot of what followed was a blur. I had become so used to moving and starting again with strangers that finding myself in a new place was becoming as normal as outgrowing childhood clothes. I wasn't even a teen-ager when I arrived at Carmen's, but I felt much older. I was realising that I had to be strong.

Returning to Carmen's didn't feel like a homecoming. When we reached her quiet, residential Peckham road, lined with semi-detached houses, my mood was low. It was dismal. With sunken shoulders, I summoned a smile and walked inside with my luggage. Mr Patel saw me off and, once again, Carmen pointed me in the direction of the bedroom I was to live in. This would be my space, my life, for the foreseeable.

In my room, I lay on the bed in deep reflection. No tears. Just numbness. Nothing. I thought about the noise and chaos of the Roseberry Street boys. For some reason, I couldn't admit to myself what Myles meant to me and how I might grow to miss him. He was the man who got me into school. Part of me thought that maybe he genuinely believed in me. Maybe he saw something good in me. I'd never told him, but he was the closest thing to a father I had ever known. And while I didn't think that he saw me as a son, he did look out for me. But still, I had left Roseberry now. I had to move on. This was a system that fractured the bonds we tried to make.

While I knew Myles and the professionals saw it as a positive thing that Carmen took me in, I struggled, as a child, to understand why she did it. In those initial days and weeks of moving back in, she didn't seem pleased to have me around and just as it had been during my probation period with her, we didn't talk much. I tiptoed blindly in the orbit of this new family, unsure of how to belong.

I had earned this place at Carmen's by being well-behaved and compliant. (Even then, I knew it was harder for Black boys to be fostered and near impossible for us to be adopted.) I was one of the lucky ones. But now that I was in this foster home, how long could I keep up the act of perfection? How long until the inevitable happened – Carmen letting me go, realising that I wasn't all she expected.

At first, I continued attending Galleywall Primary School.

'Ash, how come I don't see you around our area any more? How come we don't play out?' Jack asked me one day.

My mind raced with panic. How the hell would I begin to explain to him that I'd moved to a foster home with a new set of people? Jack had a cosy home with his parents. He had an idyllic front garden with a trimmed hedge, he had family over at Christmas and, most of all, he never had to face the fear of being let go. He was loved and couldn't possibly relate to my version of 'family life'. He'd never understand the kind of rejection I had to live with; he'd never had to audition for acceptance by a potential foster parent. Trying to explain things to him would only ruin his view of me because he wouldn't understand.

I took the easy route with my reply. 'I live with my aunty in Peckham now,' I said.

'Ah, mate. Why? Will you still be able to come play out with me on weekends?'

'Sure. I'll let you know,' I replied dismissively.

My heart sank, though. I loved hanging out with him and the others. I was already missing knock down ginger on the local council estate, and the occasional kickabout in football cages. Regardless of how I felt, though, there was no way Carmen would let me take the bus from Nunhead, Peckham to South Bermondsey alone. She had the restrictive rules of social services to abide by. I wasn't really hers, after all.

However, Carmen did allow me to play out on the few streets surrounding her house, although given that I didn't know anyone in the area, that felt solitary.

When it came to school-mates, sleepovers were off the table, too. Carmen explained that if I wanted to stay at someone's house over the weekend, their family would need to undergo background checks, which she said would be carried out by my social worker. To be honest, I couldn't think of anything more humiliating than having to tell a friend that my social worker, Mr Patel, had to investigate them and their family for a simple sleepover. I just stopped asking to do stuff with my friends. I stopped trying to be normal. I accepted that, on many levels, I wasn't like them. And it was easier to just say no to things. That way, I wouldn't have to give an account of my life as a care kid.

For some reason, at Carmen's, I grew even more ashamed of being a looked-after child. I grew increasingly conscious of how different my home life was to other people's. I didn't tell people at Galleywall about the abandonment and loneliness I often felt. I didn't tell them that I had lost touch with Myles. I just blagged it. Only Halle, my teacher, knew, although she never brought it up or made me feel uncomfortable. She just remained a teacher who, somehow, made me feel as safe as I could, given the circumstances.

Being at Galleywall, following the move to Carmen's, became difficult. Roseberry Street was a short walk from the school, yet that too felt like a distant memory. Most days, when Carmen picked me up from school in her car, I'd peer down the road that led to Roseberry, wondering which boys still lived there. Who had moved on? Did Myles or any of the boys remember me? Probably not. It wouldn't be long until that home forgot about me. I was convinced of that. It was more of an institution than a family.

Perhaps the most curious and exciting part of moving to Carmen's was having an older brother figure in her son, Reece.

For all Carmen's solemnity, Reece, when he was around, brought an energy and dynamism to that house that made everything a bit more thrilling. To the little boy I was, everything he did seemed cool.

He was an Arsenal supporter and garage-music head. So Solid Crew, Oxide & Neutrino, Dizzee Rascal and other MCs would blast from his bedroom daily. And alongside the music, was the swarm of friends and girls who would pass through.

Reece's mates referred to him as a sweet boy – a ladies' man. With his signature clean shape-up and impeccable swag – Nike tracksuit and trainers – he had a natural charm. A bunch of teenage boys his age, all in tracksuits, smoking weed (when they thought no one would notice) and taking the piss out of Reece in the living room, was a regular feature of life at Carmen's. He gave as good as he got. Their banter reminded me of Roseberry.

'Ashley. Imma teach you how to have game with chicks, you know!' he said to me over a game of Donkey Kong on the Nintendo.

I felt warm inside. It was as if there was something a bit big-brotherly in the way he wanted to take me under his wing. Our time playing computer games together was when I got to know him most. I learned that Reece had an older brother, Harvey, who lived away from home, but he didn't visit much when I first moved in.

I think Reece liked having someone to play computer games with. He was out most of the time, but on the random evening he was home, we'd play the Nintendo while Carmen cooked her irresistible chicken noodles for dinner, and it soon felt homely. I looked up to Reece. That was undeniable.

Reece didn't go to church, but Carmen wasn't having any sort of refusal from me. In the first few weeks of having moved to hers permanently, going to church was one of the things I dreaded the most. It felt stale and unrelatable.

The Sunday morning drives to pick up Carmen's elderly friend Josephine felt suffocating. I preferred the bass of Reece's garage music to the hymns and brass band of the Sunday morning choir. And what was most unsettling about church was having to drift through a sea of unknown people with a fake smile.

Joyce was a Christian, too, but her expression of her spirituality always felt warm and familiar to me. She went to a Black-majority church with gospel music. I'd get up to mischief with Conor in the pews as Joyce stood in prayer. I was adored by her doting elderly friends and, crucially, plied with sweets and treats. I was a part of that community.

At the Salvation Army, however, I felt like an infiltrator. The weird hats and suits the adults wore, emblazoned with the S, looked bizarre at best. The bulk of the kids were posh, accompanied by their mummies and daddies. I didn't know what 'middle class' was back then, but this was it. Even at such a young age, I sensed that their lives were worlds apart from my reality.

After one particular service, a man who appeared to be in his early twenties approached me. He was white, slim-built and fully clad in the 'Sally Army' uniform.

'Hi, mate, I'm Tim! I see you've been coming to church with Carmen for a while.'

'Yes. I live with her,' I replied in a subdued manner. I gave no eye contact. He was a bit too jolly for that time of the morning.

Tim explained that he played the trumpet and was a pastor for the youth in the church. 'If you're ever keen, mate, we have a youth service here on Sunday evenings. It's more chilled and everyone dresses casually. If Carmen would allow it, you could come and check it out?' he said while giving an affectionate nod to Carmen.

'Oh, okay. Yes,' I replied while thinking, no bloody way! Never. No. I cringed internally.

In the church foyer, after service, was when Carmen was her chattiest. Accompanied by me and Josephine, she'd talk with others about her work as a carer for the elderly or some plan to attend a midweek church thing with another congregant. One of the few Black people around, Carmen was effortlessly comfortable in the sea of white people at this church.

I quietly despaired, knowing that this life was now my reality. But that's the thing about being a foster kid; you don't get to choose or shape the world you exist in. It's chosen for you. At least until you're eighteen.

After church, Carmen would drop Josephine off and then we'd go back home. Reece would often just be waking up. At some point in the afternoon, we'd have Sunday dinner. A spread of roast chicken, rice and peas and other vegetables.

On the occasions when it was just me and Carmen eating at the table, we didn't talk much. Maybe because I was so young? But during the Sunday lunches when Reece was around, he injected an energy that sparked Carmen. Whether it was fondly disapproving of some scenario that Reece was regaling her with or passionately reminiscing on family memories from before my time, Carmen would show a lightness and joy that I didn't get to see when it was just us.

During those lunches with Reece, I'd sit as a silent witness to the love and companionship of a mother and her real son. I didn't know how to insert myself into these light family conversations; I didn't have funny stories or witty remarks. I didn't know the majority of people mentioned and I wasn't often given the context. Maybe I should have asked more questions or laughed at the jokes I didn't understand. I wish I hadn't felt the rejection and isolation that I did in those moments. I clearly didn't know how to do the whole family thing well, and in the absence of being involved, I sat in uncomfortable silence.

The dinner table was traumatic for me. Sitting with Carmen and Reece was a reminder of the thing

I didn't really have: a family. That couldn't be forced or faked. But still, I sucked it up. I remembered the things Myles had said – how lucky I was to now have some sort of family; that some of the other boys at Roseberry weren't considered for foster care. My current woes were nothing compared to the reality of where I could end up.

A couple of months into life at Carmen's, at the start of the summer holidays, Mr Patel came to visit.

'Ashley, I'm pleased that the meet-ups with your mother are going well. As a result, I have decided that she can take you on a whole day out. She says she wants to take you to a theme park – Chessington World of Adventures,' Mr Patel said. And my first full day out with Mum was to be unsupervised.

I jumped inside and outwardly leaped for joy. For once, my inner feelings and outer expression were consistent with each other!

Good news felt good. I drew a calendar with colouring pencils to count down the days and stuck it on the inside of my bedroom wardrobe. Carmen never disapproved of my dates with my mum, but she certainly didn't affirm them. Whereas Joyce would always speak positively about my mum, Carmen just didn't mention her. So I kept my excitement to myself.

It was a beautiful, warm day when my mother arrived at Carmen's to pick me up. Standing outside the house ready to whisk me off, she had that vulnerable, anxious look that I'd first seen at the Wimpy. As ever, Carmen didn't have many words. I assumed this was their first meeting. Even as a boy, I thought their exchange felt frosty.

'So, can you have him back by six this evening?' Carmen said.

'Absolutely, Carmen. Thank you so much,' Mum said courteously.

Very swiftly, I said goodbye to Carmen and left her house, holding my mum's hand as we set off for the train station. Her touch felt both foreign and familiar. Touch from an adult was a rarity. And at Carmen's, just like at Roseberry, hugs were non-existent.

'Hi, darling. I've missed you!' my mum said softly.

Walking with her, in unfiltered sunshine, I instantly felt lighter. We walked briskly through the streets of Nunhead, my mum's perfume permeating the air. For a day, I could forget about having to get by at Carmen's. I could forget about pretending. Maybe I could just be a kid . . . enjoy the park rides and laugh carelessly.

Today, it was just us. No glance from Mr Patel at a distance. No thirty-minute timer. Free from the invigilation of social services. Free from judgement.

Today, I was a son.

'Ashley, do you remember my friend Tanya? The one I brought to Roseberry Street? Well, she's coming with her kids. They're really excited to meet you,' Mum exclaimed. It was refreshing to hear her in such high spirits. Unlike our chats at the Wimpy, I wasn't having to worry about whether she'd burst out in tears.

Even getting a train from the local station to central London was thrilling. I rarely got on trains. But it reminded me that the world was bigger than Carmen's; it was bigger than my social workers and foster placements. This train was taking me somewhere new – and maybe, one day, life would, too.

After switching between a few trains, we eventually arrived. A sign read 'Chessington World of Adventures', and a whirl of colours and fantastical images plastered the bustling entrance area of the theme park.

'Woohooo. Hello, love!' someone shouted.

'Hiya, Tanya!' my mum replied. And a short distance away, through the busy crowd, were Tanya, a man and two children. We made our way over to them.

After some introductions to her family, Tanya handed us the tickets, and we scurried with excitement through the barriers inside. A rush of fairground noises, rides and colours overwhelmed my senses. The kid inside came alive. I was ready to have fun.

Tanya's daughter, Alicia, was a similar age to me. This was a big deal for her, too. 'I want to go on the water ride,' she said pointing, as she looked at Tanya, her mum. With her olive skin and plaits, she oozed a bubbly confidence.

We made our way over to the ride, our anticipation beginning to build.

Many of the fun things that other kids took for granted required, for me, permission from social workers and were fraught with hazards. It meant foster carers and social workers were often reluctant to allow me to do anything involving the remotest sense of adventure or risk. But today, my mum allowed me to do everything.

As we navigated the theme park, I observed other kids running around with their families in sheer delight. I looked up at my mum who was trying to gauge where the water ride was located. She knitted her eyebrows as she scoured a map. And that's when it occurred to me: today, I *was* one of the regular kids. I was 'normal'.

After queuing for what felt like an eternity, Alicia and I got on a ride. It was an epic slide that drenched us in water. In the aftermath, we shrieked with laughter. A broad smile spread across my face as I looked at Alicia in delight.

I glimpsed my mum watching me, brimming with happiness. Wet through from the ride, surrounded by my mum and her friends . . . *my* friends . . . this was the moment I never knew I needed. Is this what true family felt like?

Laughing, I began to flick water at Alicia, who was now attempting to dry her hair with a towel.

'Stop,' she moaned. 'I'll tell your mum!'

Those words stopped me in my tracks and the warmest joy filled my insides. This was the first time someone had threatened to tell on me to my mum. It felt foreign. It felt nice. Because in that moment, I was just a regular child with a regular mum. It was a moment that was something of a distant wish when I'd lived at Joyce's. When I'd gazed at the photo of my mum, hoping that one day I could be a regular son in her presence.

The majority of the day was spent lining up in mammoth queues for rides. After a bite to eat, we decided to get a photo at the theme park's makeshift photo set which was manned by a photographer. Having dressed up in cowboy regalia, we then posed.

My mum got me a printed copy of our photo. I gazed at it. We had huge smiles. I looked proud in my cowboy hat and waistcoat. For once, I didn't feel like the odd one out in the group photo. I felt a belonging and closeness to my mum that allowed me to forget about the weight of trying to be Carmen's foster son.

This was the best day of my life.

The day flew by. And, in what seemed like no time, me and Mum were back on Carmen's street, walking up to her front door.

'Mum, I don't want to go. I don't like it at Carmen's,' I said in desperation.

'Don't worry, babes. Please don't be upset. It's good for you to be there. I promise we'll go out again soon. I love you, son.'

I feigned a smile as I made my way into Carmen's house. After I parted with my mum, there was still an afterglow. A small light was lit inside. I had a mum and a bunch of people who were like family, who I'd see again. I told myself they gave me a reason to be hopeful about my life.

It was during that summer that I was told I'd no longer be able to go to Galleywall.

'Ashley, it's becoming really hard for me to drive you to school every day before work. I know you love Galleywall, but with the help of Mr Patel I've been able to find a nearer school for you to attend. It's called Riverton Primary, and you'll start in September, after the summer.'

Another decision I had no say in. I didn't respond. A lot of our communication consisted of Carmen giving instructions and me being compliant.

Leaving Galleywall meant ending my friendships with Kaseem and Jack. I knew I wouldn't see them after that. I wouldn't see Halle again.

I left Galleywall with no suspensions. No record of misbehaviour. It was the place that taught me to enjoy school and, perhaps, to even give learning a shot. That said, it didn't seem to matter how good Galleywall was for me – Riverton Primary School was much nearer, and distance was what seemed important to Carmen.

I attended Riverton for my final year of primary school. Mrs Sharp was my teacher. I seemed to fit into my new class quickly. Shaq, Solomon, Lee and Vivek were boys I grew to become friendly with. But the streak of settled behaviour that I had demonstrated at Galleywall quickly evaporated.

There was a kid in my new class called Baz who I didn't click with. Or perhaps, feeling I had to prove myself, I saw him as someone I could muster some authority over to gain respect from the other kids.

Quite soon after I started at Riverton, we were taken to the local library for a school trip. As the librarian was reading our class a book, I noticed Baz, who was white, with short blond hair, gazing at me venomously. Or so it seemed to me.

As we all sat cross-legged, looking at the friendly woman who was sat on a chair reading to us, I shouted over to Baz, 'Who you looking at?'

'Ah, shut up, you mug,' he replied dismissively.

In a fit of embarrassment and childish rage, I jumped over to where he sat and began to throw punches at his face. He fought back. We rolled across the library floor for what couldn't have been that long, exchanging blows, until Mrs Sharp, her teaching assistant and the library staff dragged us apart. The rest of the class erupted and jeered in excitement and shock until Mrs Sharp shouted them into silence.

Heaving and out of breath, I was soon taken back to school where I was kept in Mrs Hedgeway's (the head teacher's) office. Carmen was asked to pick me up and upon her arrival, I was swiftly given notice of a week's suspension. I felt humiliated.

I didn't know how Carmen would react. I didn't expect anger from her – more likely rejection, if anything. She said nothing on the short drive home. Then she acted like she did any other evening. We had dinner. I washed the dishes. A bit of telly. She didn't mention the incident once. I didn't even have to apologise. I knew that Reece had been suspended on numerous occasions. Maybe she was used to this sort of thing.

Regardless, though, I didn't need Carmen to tell me off to feel bad. I had broken the spell of good behaviour that I'd begun at Galleywall. So early on at Riverton, I was already creating the wrong name for myself.

What would Halle or Myles have said? I missed them. I missed Galleywall. I even missed Roseberry. But as I didn't have an outlet for these feelings, I buried it all inside. Kept it to myself. Maybe my suppressed emotion partly explains why, in a library of all places, I jumped on another kid and pelted them in the face.

Six months into life at Carmen's, I was fed up. Fed up with the ongoing silence of her home; fed up with the Sally Army; and fed up with my new school.

But as time dragged on, I continued to reluctantly go to church with her. And week after week, Tim, the youth pastor, pursued me about going to the evening youth service. Finally, one particular evening, Carmen insisted I go. It was non-negotiable. Maybe it was to shut Tim up, or maybe she wanted to try and convert me, but she wasn't taking no for an answer. And so, as with many things to do with life at Carmen's, I went because I had to.

It was a six-thirty start in the evening. Carmen walked me to the front of the Salvation Army where, in a bit of a sulk, I coolly made my way in by myself.

Kids in their early and mid-teens, dressed in normal clothes, loitered outside the church. To my relief, no one was in that awkward church uniform. I sauntered around the foyer, where more young people were milling about, a few of them even seeming a bit rowdy.

Eventually, I stood awkwardly in a corner, not knowing who to talk to. I spotted some of the kids from the morning services who normally wore the uniforms, but didn't feel like talking to any of them. Then there were other kids who weren't part of the normal church – who seemed more local from around Nunhead and Peckham. Normal young people. There were more Black kids there, too.

Taking a big gulp, I edged into the church hall. I looked around, taking everything in. Compared to the mornings, it was dark. The hall was spotted with a few additional dimmed stage lights. Rather than brass instruments scattering the platform, electric guitars and a keyboard had prominence. And where chairs were normally placed for the morning churchgoers they were now cleared away, the hall's floor instead covered with pillows and rugs.

This set-up felt more like a bar than a church (not that I'd been to a lot of bars). Perhaps this was Tim's strategy for appealing to reluctant youth like me. Nevertheless, this relaxed front couldn't fool me. Underneath the vibes of normalcy, these people were still odd and unrelatable. That was still my overriding impression.

As I looked around, taking in the people and the setting, Tim called out to me. 'Ashley, you're here!' he chirped as he made his way over.

I was startled that he wasn't wearing his uniform. Instead, he had on just a regular pair of jeans and a T-shirt.

As he took me to sit with him, some trendy-looking musicians took their places on the platform, ready for the church service to start. I was still unhappy about being there but now also mildly curious, unsure of what to expect next.

All of a sudden, the musicians began to play and a drumbeat and bassline pulsated through the air. The young people began to groove. This felt more like a concert. I looked around in confusion, like a lost sheep. The band then threw in some electric guitars and pop-sounding vocals. Things were now well under way. Although the lyrics were religious and worshipful, the format was quite contemporary. I didn't know how to react. I didn't know whether to take the piss or nod in engagement. I just watched. I beheld this diverse group of youths in hoodies, jeans and tracksuits, playing the most unconventional religious music I'd ever known. It was a far cry from the morning service Carmen always dragged me to.

Tim was in his element as he looked around at the crowd of fifty or so young people. Soon, the music stopped and everyone sat down on the cushions. Tim got up to give a 'message'. Unlike the tone of the morning services, he spoke in a more chatty, relaxed way. It was easier to engage with, to be honest.

I can't remember a lot of what he said. I phased in and out, still taking in the different people and surroundings. But at one point during his talk, as he got caught up in the power of his emotion and fervent belief, he said something that hit me unexpectedly:

'Whoever you are – you are not a mistake. God has made you for a purpose. You have meaning.' He looked around the hall intently. This was the most serious I'd seen him.

There wasn't a lot at church that I absorbed but, for some reason, those words sparked something inside of me. On some level, perhaps I did think I was a mistake. I certainly knew I was unwanted and unadoptable. But as Tim went on, it felt as if I was the only person in the room. It was as if every word was bespoke and crafted for me. I can't remember the last time someone had spoken to me so directly. My heart raced. I thought back to when Joyce let me go. My eyes watered, but I tried to hold it all together.

Just moments before, this whole set-up had seemed like a corny, unrelatable church thing that had no significance for me. But now, because of a few mere sentences, I felt as if my insides had been exposed. The affirmation that I was not a mistake could have been the message I had been waiting to hear ever since I was shunted into the care system.

But was it true? Was there a man upstairs, a god, who thought someone like me had significance? Did my life really matter to anyone? Or was it too good to be true? Bullshit?

As Tim finished speaking and the service came to a close, I kept my thoughts inside, barely saying anything. When Carmen came to pick me up, we walked home, and she looked at me.

'How was it?' she asked in a rare show of genuine interest and curiosity.

'Yeah, all right,' I replied, head down.

But inside, a whirl of questions stirred. Could a life like mine really matter? I didn't care about religion.

I wasn't scared of hell and was too preoccupied with down here to care about an afterlife. All I wanted to know was whether my life had meaning – whether I mattered to someone.

Over time, I tried to make sense of this new life, which I certainly never volunteered for. A life split between Carmen's, church and my new primary school.

The more I got to know the boys at Riverton, the more aware I became of the fact that where I lived – Nunhead – was slap bang in the middle of two rival crews: the Peckham boys and Ghetto boys.

Through chats in the playground, I learned that boys who were just a few years older – in their early teens and upwards – were involved in the kind of drugs, violence and risk that Myles had always warned me about avoiding. Maybe that's why sending me to school was so important to him.

Some of the boys in my class at Riverton would boast about knowing some of the Ghetto boys – essentially, certain kids who lived within the New Cross postcode. Despite being right next to Peckham, the two crews were aggressively opposed to each other and rarely ventured into each other's territories.

One classmate would often brag about the antics his older brother got up to with the Ghetto boys. He'd talk wildly about his brother carrying a shank and the clashes he'd have with boys from Peckham. To us boys listening in the playground, the brother's heroism was something we could only dream of.

Back at Carmen's, when Reece and his mates would hang out in the living room, they'd often cuss the Peckham boys, but it was only as I became more aware of the reality of these crews through the chats at Riverton that I understood that Reece, the foster brother I secretly looked up to, was actually a Ghetto boy.

If anything, as a young boy in care, this made me respect him even more. I knew what abandonment and rejection felt like. I knew only too well, what it felt like to be uprooted and torn from the ones you love. A gang of boys to rely on, fight for and protect was the sort of community and family that I found enviable as a young, insecure foster boy. I would have done anything for a band of brothers who'd have my back.

But one night, my view of Reece's world changed.

9

UNFORGETTABLE WORDS

'Ashley, wake up!'

It was well after midnight when Carmen turned on my light and hurried me out of bed. There was an urgency in her voice I'd never heard before.

'We're going to the hospital. Reece is there.'

I was concerned and confused. Reece was where? A hospital?

Carmen threw a coat over her pyjamas and, with her headscarf still on, made her way to the car. I followed behind. We drove to the hospital and dashed to A & E.

We were swiftly taken to a room where Reece lay on a hospital bed, covered in bandages. Blood was splattered over his face.

A woman introduced herself as a doctor and motioned us to sit down. Her tone was sober. We were told that Reece had got caught up in a violent altercation and one of his boys had brought him to the hospital. Reece had been struck repeatedly on the face with a glass bottle. He had lost one of his front teeth and as my eyes frantically scanned him, I could see that he also had a wound on his head.

'Fortunately, he has no life-threatening injuries. He's lucky to be okay,' said the doctor.

I'm not sure why but I felt emotion. Was I sad? Scared for him? Was this how people felt when loved ones were in pain? I stood there motionless, trying to grasp what exactly was going on.

Reece was awake. Clearly in pain, but wearing his familiar cheeky grin. He was advised not to talk by the doctor.

I could see Carmen was relieved that the injuries weren't too serious. She enquired about the person who carried out the attack, but the doctor had no information.

We stayed there for a while. I waited outside Reece's room for much of it. During the early hours of that morning, he had his tooth reinserted.

Soon the doctor left Reece to rest for a bit. When I entered his room, he and Carmen were deep in conversation. Carmen made some disparaging remarks about his friends, saying that they were no good for him.

I mumbled a sheepish hello to Reece; he nodded at me, appearing to be in good spirits.

'Ash, that doctor's buff, innit!' he said brightly.

I laughed. I was glad that he was okay. I didn't tell him that, though. Just smiled. Feeling like an outsider with this family, it was hard to know how to position myself in this scenario; I didn't know what to say, or how to feel.

Over time, and through a series of chats that I overheard between him and his mates, I discovered that it was a Peckham boy who'd bottled him. He had been on the wrong turf while out on a date, and the attack was the price he paid. He and his mates vowed to mash up the boy who did this to him.

Even back then, I knew that Reece was lucky to be alive. And I soon discovered that there was nothing glamorous or heroic about what happened to him. As much as I wanted a crew, a family – the acceptance and approval of a gang were not worth my life. After all, if my life did have meaning, as Tim had said, I wanted to see what that actually meant.

Eventually, I finally met Carmen's other son, Harvey. He was in his twenties – some years older than Reece. Only when Harvey was around with his toddler son, Malachi, did Reece stop giving off the confidence and swagger that seemed to come to him so naturally.

Broad, lean and dark-skinned, Harvey had a rugged appearance, possibly due to his stubbly facial hair. He had a small Afro and was easily six foot tall. I didn't know much about his life outside Carmen's house. I wasn't privy to those details and I knew better than to ask. Whereas I looked up to Reece, with Harvey I felt an intrinsic intimidation. I didn't say much around him. Avoided eye contact.

Exchanges between Harvey, Carmen and Reece were rarely warm. I was too young to understand the brotherly dynamic, but I knew things weren't right between them. Reece would often pop out when Harvey visited for the odd Sunday dinner. Yet Harvey brought a lot of joy to Carmen's home through Malachi. He couldn't have been any older than three. He was mixed-race like me, with a Black dad and white mum – also like me.

Carmen doted on Malachi. I also loved it when he was around. He didn't view me as fostered. He didn't 'other' me. He simply played with me, giggled with me, just like he did with his real family. He didn't differentiate between me and them.

Carmen often looked after Malachi on Saturdays. He and I would sprawl on the carpet in front of the telly, goofing around with toys, and generally having fun. There was an ease and bliss that came with playing with Malachi. Maybe it was the fact that I didn't have to pretend to be anyone else. I didn't have to impress him.

The simple joy of those Saturday antics brought a rare sense of contentment. The smell of Carmen's seasoned chicken would permeate the house, and when Reece was in, garage music would blare from his room as he freshened up, ready to head out.

As Malachi and I got up to boyish mischief, the vibe fused to create a sense of family and normality that I mostly went without. Despite being younger and barely able to string a sentence together, Malachi offered acceptance. His high-pitched giggle and cheeky smile were the greatest signs that he was happy and enjoyed playing with me. In his eyes, I belonged.

One Saturday afternoon, Carmen, Malachi and I had just come back home from grocery shopping at the local Rye Lane Market. Carmen made her way to the kitchen to prepare food and I took up my usual place in the living room with Malachi, assuming a bit of responsibility for him when it was just the two of us. We were playing tag and he was laughing hysterically as I relentlessly chased him.

Although Carmen had firmly laid out the parameters for our antics – the living-room carpet – Malachi waddled out of the living room to the passageway. I followed, calling out, between laughs, 'Malachi, stay in the living room. You're not allowed out there.'

Suddenly, as he turned a corner out of the door, Malachi slipped and fell over, banging his head on the wall. The thump of Malachi's head hitting the wall stopped my laughter instantly. There was a moment of silence, followed by an incessant wave of crying and wailing from Malachi. He lay there on the floor of the passageway, looking up at me in tears.

I froze, staring back. Then, after a few moments, Malachi sat up, still crying, but to my relief, he was okay.

Carmen rushed out of the kitchen and stormed down the passageway towards us, shouting 'Malachi!' Then, 'What happened?' she asked sharply, directing her gaze at me.

Now sitting next to Malachi on the floor, I looked up at her sheepishly. 'Sorry, it was a mistake,' I muttered.

There was a slight pause, then, 'Your whole life is a mistake,' she snapped back.

We locked eyes and then, after a swift assessment of Malachi to check he was okay, she made her way back to the kitchen.

Things were a blur from there. The brutal impact of those words ricocheted through me like bullets through flesh. I sat there for ages. Was I a mistake?

In that moment, I didn't cry. I didn't respond at all. But inside, a dam of despair had broken. For all the delusion I held about being a part of Malachi's family, Carmen's words confirmed a different story. I was, at best, a mistake. A mistake who would somehow make his way through this punishment called childhood, hoping for the love of strangers in a broken system.

The foster kid that I was, I knew the sting of rejection all too well. But even so, Carmen's words cut deeply. I honestly hadn't meant any harm to Malachi, I repeatedly reassured myself. And while he eventually got back to his bubbly, playful disposition, for the rest of that Saturday, I didn't play.

So my suspicions were right. And Tim, the pastor, was wrong. He was chatting bullshit. How could a life like mine have meaning when even the woman looking after me thought I was a mistake? So much for her Christianity.

I was worried about how Harvey would react to finding out that Malachi had bumped his head because of me. And most likely, I thought, Carmen would ask social services to move me on. I was no longer compatible with her family. The suspension from Riverton was one thing. But now this? I certainly didn't meet her expectations. Maybe I should have stayed at Roseberry Street and waited to be moved on to another care home.

I didn't know where I'd end up, but I now knew it was only a matter of time until life at Carmen's would come to an end. And, honestly, that thought came as a relief to me. I wanted to be a mistake somewhere else.

The year I spent at Riverton was my last at primary school.

Thanks to Myles I hadn't fallen behind academically and was able to progress year by year, even if my behaviour was still a problem. I didn't know it back then, but if he hadn't forced me to go to school when I was at Roseberry, I would have likely ended up in a pupil-referral unit, or out of education completely.

For all the coldness I often felt at Carmen's, I knew she, like Myles, cared about school, and it was because of her that I landed a spot at Bacon's College – a secondary state school in south Bermondsey. I was due to start after the summer holidays.

But before the new term kicked off, Carmen organised a trip to New York and, by some miracle, convinced social services to pay for me to go, too. It marked my first trip abroad. And the day Mr Patel told me about it, I was secretly very happy.

It would be me, Reece and Carmen spending a couple of weeks in New York with relatives of theirs who lived out there – apparently, some aunty figure to Reece and his cousins. I didn't know for sure if the woman was Carmen's sister. I must admit, though, it felt nice – and also surprising – to be included in Carmen's family holiday plans.

After what seemed like an eternity of travel, we arrived at the airport in New York where we were picked up by the woman and her three children – one my age and the other two older. We would be staying with them for the duration of our two-week holiday.

As we drove through New York, I gazed at the bigness of everything, knowing I was lucky to be abroad with a foster family. Most kids in my position didn't get to see much outside of their local borough or area.

For those two weeks, I saw Carmen come alive around her relatives. This was a holiday of summer barbecues in the Bronx with food laced with spices and seasoning, family board games and stories of nostalgia.

Yet as grateful as I was to be there and as much as I tried to fit in, I couldn't help but feel a distance and dislocation. Something about living with another group of strangers abroad, even if just for a holiday, felt not dissimilar to starting again at a new home as a care kid.

I didn't really belong. And despite Carmen's relatives' best efforts to include me, I don't think they would have missed me if I wasn't there. I wasn't part of this family. I was an add-on – an accessory.

Nevertheless, time flew by. Maybe I should've got out of my head and been more appreciative of the holiday, which included a visit to Times Square and a viewing of the Rockefeller building.

Ever since my short-term suspension from Riverton, I'd thought Carmen would kick me out. But even with the disconnection I sometimes felt in the Big Apple, maybe Carmen on some level did see me as a part of her family? Questions like these around belonging increasingly plagued me as a boy, and I'd oscillate often between hoping I was accepted and being convinced that no one really gave a shit.

Before I knew it, the summer holidays were soon coming to an end. Back at Carmen's, in south London, I began preparing for secondary school. Being in south Bermondsey, Bacon's College was quite near Roseberry Street, and I wondered if maybe I'd bump into Myles or one of the boys from the home. Since being at Carmen's I'd completely lost contact with them all.

Carmen had gone to the trouble of buying my school uniform. On the morning of my first day, I remember being in my bedroom, throwing on the sharp blue blazer over my white shirt and tie. The school's emblem, a yellow lion, was embroidered on one side of the blazer.

Getting ready that morning, I was nervous, unsure of what to expect. What would the other students be like? As a year seven, I'd be at the bottom of the ladder. How would the older students treat us newbies? What were the teachers like? And how would I tell others that I was fostered?

This was yet another new beginning. Another home. Like all the other times, I'd learn the moves and find a way to get by. If I'd been able to start again after being let go by Joyce, then I could probably start a secondary school. As for not getting in trouble, though? Well, I couldn't be sure about that.

At some point while I was getting ready, Carmen sternly chivvied me along. 'Ashley, hurry up now. Do you wanna be late?' she called out.

I rushed downstairs. Carmen was at the bottom, looking up at me. Her expression lightened as she beheld me. She didn't say anything. Just looked. Was that a look of pride I saw on her face? Was she proud of me?

I swung my rucksack over my shoulder and made my way out of the house. Carmen paused and insisted she take a photo of me. Taking a small camera out of her bag, she knelt down to my level and snapped away as I stood outside her front door. A photo for my first day of secondary school.

Carmen confused me. I didn't understand her. One day she'd called me a mistake; the next, she was flying me to New York and capturing pictures of me in my new school uniform. I just didn't know where I stood. On an average day, I assumed she didn't really care about me and was, maybe, just looking after me to get money from social services. But then there were moments – like this one – that made me wonder if she did actually care. After all, she went to all the effort to get me into a new school, and was looking at me fondly on my first day, even if she'd never admit it.

Bacon's was a fairly modern and impressive-looking secondary school. The reception area was spacious and was where we fresh-faced year sevens were sorted into our tutor groups. We then filed along behind teachers as we were led to our new classrooms and spaces, while older students looked on. Fresh meat, they probably thought, as we passed through the school corridors.

Starting this school was not dissimilar to starting at Roseberry Street. No parental figures, just guardians and a bunch of young people I would have to learn to integrate with. When it came to the real rules of survival, you had to learn them yourself.

Despite my records of suspension and being fostered, I was surprised to find that I was placed in one of the top academic sets in the year. This was something the school decided based on a reading test I had done in the weeks leading up to the start of term. I'd never thought I was particularly smart (although Joyce had always commented on my intelligence), so being placed in a high set was a form of affirmation I'd rarely encountered.

Finally, was there a bit of hope?

10

OLD AND NEW HABITS

Over the course of the first weeks and months at Bacon's, I gradually grew accustomed to life at my new secondary school. I found the mix of new subjects, students and teachers exciting. Immersing myself into new worlds of learning and ideas gave me a buzz that I hadn't experienced before. The most captivating for me was music.

I still remember my first music lesson. All the year sevens filed into a classroom full of keyboards, percussion and other instruments. Rather than sitting at desks, we each sat at a keyboard with a computer. I looked at the keyboard notes in astonishment and thought about the music I heard at the church youth service, which I still continued to attend. It was that music, after all, which had opened me to the idea of church.

I was normally chatty in class and often tended to distract others when I got bored. In this music room, though, I was completely enthralled by the equipment around me. And then there was the music teacher – a Black man with glasses, small in stature and with a warm and friendly demeanour.

'Hello, and welcome to music! I'm Mr Tunbridge, and this year, I'll be your teacher,' he announced.

Instantly, I felt complete safety and assurance in his class. Early on in the lesson, Mr Tunbridge took to a keyboard and began to play and sing. From his mouth came the most soulful vocal. I was mesmerised. I forgot about the other kids; I dropped my bravado and just watched in complete awe.

He then stood up and began to stroll slowly around the classroom gazing at us intently. 'As well as learning theory and history behind music, in my class, you will discover the power of music,' he explained. 'The power of sound, the power of music, has the potential to inspire. It can move us, and even heal us. I want you to find your unique sound and passion for music.'

Mr Tunbridge spoke with a conviction that felt almost supernatural. 'If I can help you find a passion for music this year, I'll have done my job.' Every word seemed true and heartfelt.

I didn't say a word to him during that lesson. I just listened. But it was the most inspiring lesson I'd ever experienced in my eleven years of life.

For once, I really cared about making a good impression at school. In every lesson, I listened, concentrated and did my best. School felt like a new universe, a fresh start, away from the label of being a 'foster kid'. I was beginning to realise that my ability to do well didn't have to be determined by my start in life. Doing well at school was about escaping my reality of the care system. That's how I viewed things – at least until a few weeks in.

It was during a drama class that I clashed with another student, called Gregory. Our task was to do some sort of role play. After an unmemorable, crappy performance from me, Gregory started to take the mickey. And in a spontaneous attempt to protect my own honour, I shot across to him and began to punch him in the face. Just like at Riverton at the library. The class began to shout. Gregory fought back. Not only did the drama teacher attempt to pull us apart, but within moments, Mr Tunbridge, the music teacher, had also run in from his classroom to intervene.

'Ashley, come with me now!' Mr Tunbridge said with a ferocity that was surprising.

I followed him to the music room which was empty.

'What on earth was going on there?' he asked with concern.

I went on to explain how Gregory was mocking my drama thing which led me to fight him.

'Ashley, that's not the behaviour we expect here. I'm disappointed and we will have to suspend you. But I hope you can learn from this and move on.'

From there, I expected to be sent to the head teacher's office, but Mr Tunbridge had a different idea. 'Ashley, how about you stay here for the rest of the period and practise on one of the keyboards? I'll be in my office, but you can stay here if you want.'

'Er, okay. Sure,' I said awkwardly, not fully knowing what to make of the offer.

As I made my way over to a keyboard, he went through a door to his office. I put some headphones on and began to play the white and black notes, unsure of how to string a chord. As my small fingers moved across the keyboard, a wave of peace hit me. I forgot about the incident with Gregory, forgot about Carmen and foster care. I just enjoyed the sounds coming through. I felt contentment.

I was sent home for a few days on suspension. And although I was disappointed that I'd been suspended only a few weeks into starting Bacon's, the impact of playing that keyboard stuck with me as I made my way home on the bus. It had provided a momentary escape. Music had power.

Like the last time, Carmen didn't say much or give much of a reaction to the news of my suspension.

Not long after my suspension, I received the news that Mr Patel would no longer be my social worker. A new one, Nina, would be taking over. For me, this was just another day in the life of a foster kid. I didn't get a chance to say goodbye or to thank him for introducing me to my mum. He was just gone.

I first met Nina when she visited for our review meeting. Reviews are where social workers for both the foster child and carer visit the home accompanied by another, often more senior council worker. Besides drinking a lot of tea and making small talk, they turn up to assess how the foster placement is going. They do this while writing notes and filling in a bunch of forms. When it came to social workers assessing my life, there was always paperwork involved. I hated those meetings, and on this particular review, things were tenser than normal.

Nina had a large build, was of aboriginal heritage and had a gentleness about her. But by now, I knew better than to trust her.

'Hi, Ashley,' she began. 'I'm Nina and I've heard a lot about you. Mr Patel has had to move on, I'm afraid, but I'm really glad that I'll be your social worker from hereon in.' Nina was to the point. No need for soothing words or platitudes. I knew how things went by now.

She continued: 'I know you've had a bit of a rocky start at secondary school, but I know we can turn things around.'

I feigned a small smile.

Carmen and the professionals (a reviewing officer and two social workers) all had cups of tea in hand. It was dark outside by now, and the cold season was kicking in. Between moments of silence, each professional would chip in to try and make small talk.

'I hear New York was fun?' Carmen's social worker chimed in.

I didn't give much reaction.

Then, at some point, the tone changed and the pleasantries subsided as the senior reviewing officer, a white, older-looking woman, kicked off the official part of the meeting.

'So, Carmen. How's it all going?' she asked, legs crossed and pen in hand. She leaned in towards Carmen like those journalists on the telly do during interviews.

Carmen remained silent, looking at the ground. I knew she'd have bad stuff to say about me, especially after the suspension. I watched her, ready for whatever criticism she had to make about me. After what seemed to be a long, long silence, Carmen looked up.

'Thank you all so much for coming,' she began. Her tone was light. Pleasant. 'There have been a few events recently that have been quite challenging for me to deal with. I need some time. I've had a think and I'd like to have a two-week break from Ashley, please.'

Carmen's social worker chimed in; she seemed surprised. 'Do you mean a respite, Carmen? You want him sent to another placement temporarily?'

Carmen nodded.

My eyes darted between Carmen and her social worker as I tried to grasp every word being uttered about me. I felt invisible. There they were, speaking about me, but not one look in my direction. No regard for me. Carmen didn't make eye contact with me at all.

'Well, okay. You are entitled to respite, Carmen. We'll make the arrangements for that as soon as possible,' remarked the reviewing officer.

It was as if Carmen was asking for a refund for a dodgy hoover.

Nina asked me to leave the room for a moment. I went to my bedroom and sat on my bed, knees tucked into my chest. My eyes gazed into nothing. I can't recall feeling particularly sad. What could I feel? There was only one way this made sense to me: Carmen didn't really want me. I was a fad. Another project to allow her to fulfil her sense of Christian duty.

I could hear the professionals and Carmen in deep discussion from upstairs, although I couldn't make out the words. Then, at some point, I was called back downstairs. I wouldn't show them weakness. I wouldn't show sadness or cry or get angry. It was what it was.

I retook my seat and the professionals stared at me as if they were assessing some broken product. Carmen still didn't look at me. She didn't seem remorseful or guilty and honestly, I didn't expect any of that.

Nina spoke like some sort of mediator:

'Ashley, I know this can't be an easy thing to hear, but Carmen is doing a fantastic job caring for you and sometimes foster carers need a break.'

'Yeah, okay. Cool,' I responded. I wanted this meeting to be over. On some level, I felt humiliated.

Nina paused, perhaps expecting me to say more or give some sort of reaction. 'Well, look,' she went on. 'I'll arrange to visit you separately. We'll be sending you to your two-week respite placement as soon as possible. I'll let you know once we've found somewhere.'

As ever, I had no say in the matter. I wanted to see my mum to tell her about it, but I assumed there was no point in asking. If I'm honest, deep down, it hurt. I wouldn't admit that, though.

Soon after, the professionals left. After seeing them to the door, Carmen made her way to the kitchen to cook dinner. I listened for her footsteps, making sure she'd left the passageway before I headed upstairs and escaped to my bedroom.

I didn't know what I could say to Carmen after the meeting. Maybe I owed her an apology. Why did she want the break? This further reinforced the idea that I was a problem to her. Broken, perhaps, in some way. I felt she didn't know how to care for me. No one did. And being the boy that I was, I blamed myself.

Before the week had ended, Nina returned to explain where I'd be going for the respite. 'Ashley, we've found a foster mother for you not too far from here. In Deptford. Her name's Valerie, she's Jamaican and has a lovely son who's older. He used to go to Bacon's for secondary school, too.'

Was that little detail meant to excite me? I didn't say anything. As with all the moves that came after Joyce, I resolved not to show emotion. I would simply await my fate and stay strong.

II

AFLOAT LIKE THE MOON

In a matter of days, Nina was driving me to my two-week placement. I didn't say a proper goodbye to Carmen. I think she was just relieved to see the back of me. I didn't care, though.

We soon parked up near a block of flats on a high street. As with previous experiences of being shunted around, I didn't know what to expect. It felt like some sort of prison sentence. Nina walked me inside the block, up a couple of flights of stairs. I didn't make my anxiety or fear known, but my small hands were clammy as I clung on to my sports bag. For some reason, this shorter placement seemed even more intimidating than others. Maybe I could just lock myself away in a bedroom for two weeks, I hoped secretly. It was too much to try and settle into yet another unknown home and get used to a new bunch of people.

Nina knocked on the door of one of the flats.

A woman – Valerie – opened the door, smiling. Not particularly surprised or delighted, just courteous. She'd clearly done this respite thing before. I wasn't the first. Just another kid for a bit of cash, I thought.

Nina left me at the door. I followed Valerie down a hall, and she showed me to my bedroom. I wasn't even curious to see her home or get to know her. I just wanted to hide away and be solitary. I sat on the single bed. Alone.

Valerie gave me a bit of space and then popped back to check on me.

'Ashley, I know it's a short time, but me want you to feel comfortable.' Her Jamaican accent and broken English were similar to Joyce's. But she wasn't Joyce. 'I'm cooking some food now, and later, I'll be having some people round. That okay?'

As if I have a say in the matter, I thought to myself. I nodded.

Time drifted, and I just sat in this new bedroom. I unpacked a bit, then looked out the window. I was terrified to leave the room in case I encountered Valerie or anyone else. Fortunately, she pretty much left me to myself for those first few hours after my arrival.

It soon turned to evening. Apart from popping to the bathroom to use the toilet and grabbing some food, I remained in the bedroom. At some point, though, reggae and bashment music blared through the flat, and the pitter-patter of steps and the hum of people talking eventually filtered through the soundtrack.

This wasn't just a gathering of people; it was a party. As the hours dragged on, I listened from the confines of my bedroom to everything that was taking place beyond it. I pressed my ear to the door to determine what sounds I could make out. What were they talking about? Did anyone besides Valerie know that there was a young foster boy in the flat, in this bedroom?

The party went on late into the night, but the music was too loud for me to sleep. The pulsating bass kept me up. Eventually, my belly rumbled with hunger, to the point that I determined to try to leave my room to grab a plate of food.

Mustering up courage, I left the bedroom. As I opened the door, I was hit by the music, the scents and scenes of people in pure enjoyment. The room was absolutely packed. I walked between and through the adults who towered above me – dancing, drinking and chatting. A few people smiled at me, but I just continued scouring the place for some food. Then I bumped into Valerie.

'Ashley – you okay?' she asked. 'You comfortable?' She shouted through the music while bending down to me. A few onlookers appeared startled at the sight of me. Or maybe I was just paranoid.

'Yes. Please can I have some food?' I asked, straining to be heard.

'Of course, darling. There's some curried goat and chicken on the table over there. Have all you want.' She pointed me in the right direction.

Like a timid mouse scavenging for crumbs, I nipped over to the food, made up a plate and scurried off back to the bedroom. Closing the door behind me, I sighed a breath of relief, tucked myself into a corner on the bed and began to eat.

Looking out the bedroom window at a darkened sky, I screamed inside. Where the hell was I? Why didn't I have anyone? Why didn't I have a home?

While I'd become desensitised to all the moves, there was something about being turfed into this new placement and family party that pained me beyond words. Eating that chicken on the plastic plate, I had no bravado or strength. My throat was aching from the pain and emotion I was trying to suppress.

As the group outside the bedroom cheered the tune that had just started through the speakers, I breathed heavily, tears flowing down my face. No one could hear me through the music, but still, I cried in silence.

God, if you're real, I hope you can hear me, I said in my head.

Waking up the next morning was like a gut punch. I was unsure of where I was and who else was in this flat, besides Valerie. She didn't come to check on me. Maybe she thought it best to just leave me for a bit.

Hearing the buzz of what I thought was a telly, I eventually sheepishly emerged from the bedroom. Valerie was deep in cleaning the house from the previous night's antics.

'Morning, Ashley. You all right? You sleep well?'

'Yes, thanks,' I lied.

'I've put some cereal out for you. Help yourself.'

She then shouted for her son, Jarell, who casually and comfortably entered the living space area.

'Ashley, good to meet you, bro.'

On edge, I took a seat at the kitchen table to have some breakfast. I smiled. Didn't say much.

Jarell was a college student. Walking around in his pyjamas, he was effortlessly at ease in the comfort of his own home. I envied that. I watched him in his habitat. I felt so far away from my life at Carmen's that I could have been on the other side of the world, in a house full of people speaking another language.

Valerie was a decent person, but I'd been upended into her life and home and was just expected to get on with it. I felt like the worst of imposters. It was impossible to feel comfortable, and during my time there I did my best to be alone. I'd only watch TV in the living space if no one else was around. Still reeling from the rejection of Carmen wanting a break, it was near impossible to open myself up in this new, temporary home. It was emotionally torturous.

Before long, Monday came around and it was time for school. Valerie was going to drop me off at Bacon's for the first few days. As I got out of her car, some of the other year sevens noticed me. One of my first friends at Bacon's was Andre Phillips. He was a keen footballer and drummer, so we'd connected in the playground and the music room. Seeing me walk up to the school gate, he ran up to me.

'Is that your mum?' Andre asked, looking over at Valerie.

I quickly thought up a lie. 'No, she's family. We slept over at hers for a party.'

As I'd entered my teenage years and become more aware of being a foster child, I'd grown even more anxious at school about telling the truth about my home life. And in my teenage insecurity, I'd often overhype and create lies about my family in the hope that this would impress people. I'd maintain that I was related to famous people – whether a mixed-race footballer or popstar – in the twisted hope that I'd gain others' approval and somehow deflect from the truth. Within just a few months of starting at Bacon's, I had made claims to be related to at least half a dozen celebrities.

In truth, school eased the load of surviving this respite placement, and soon enough, the two weeks had come to an end, and I was back at Carmen's. No big hug or welcome back. A curt greeting and I was back to it. It was good to see Reece again, but honestly though, this wasn't really a welcome back, was it? Because, deep down I knew I wasn't wanted.

It's funny how our view of things changes over time.

During those first couple of years at Bacon's, suspensions were a regular feature. The odd fight, act of vandalism or rebellion would see me whisked to the headmaster's office, where I'd get served with a letter and then sent home.

Yet despite the bouts of trouble at school, there were aspects of life at Bacon's that became an escape from the struggle of being at Carmen's. I'd often find myself in the music room after school with Andre. As he played out a percussive beat, I'd be on the electric keyboard, working the notes out. In those moments, armed with our little-to-no ability, we'd play our blues away until Mr Tunbridge forced us to leave the school premises.

Looking back, I reckon the music room was the closest thing to therapy I'd ever known. Music became a way for me to channel trauma as a kid, to speak out the unsaid words of pain. It became a language that gave expression to the rejection that lurked below. And while my pal Andre may have just been killing time after school, for me, the music room felt most like home.

Over the months following the respite placement, I saw and got to know my social worker, Nina, a bit more. It was during one of her visits that I plucked up the courage to make a request.

'Nina, I really like my music lessons at school . . . I was wondering if I could get some piano lessons and maybe a keyboard to play in my bedroom? Is that the sort of thing that social workers pay for?'

I didn't really ask for things as a foster child, and I knew by then that Carmen only had a limited amount of money to spend on me – something that was allotted by social services. I asked this time, though, because I was desperate to learn how to play the piano. I braced myself for the rejection.

Nina paused, looking at me. 'Ashley, I'm really glad you like your music. However, there's quite a process that I'll have to go through to be able to sign off extra money for this sort of thing. Let me speak to my manager and see what we can do.'

At least it wasn't a 'no' from her, I thought. It annoyed me, though. Kids in regular families didn't have to go through this sort of thing. They didn't have to fight for permissions from council workers to buy simple things. They didn't have to go through systems and bureaucracy to get their parent to buy them a musical instrument. At every turn, in so many life moments, I was reminded that I was different. That I was fostered. Nothing was ever straightforward.

I knew that Nina had a job to do. I had even come to appreciate that she had people 'above' her she had to report to when it came to me and my life. I just wished that for once, a simple request could be met with a simple response.

Over time, though, I found another – unexpected – outlet for music. Church.

The band at Tim's youth church would meet up before the service started, and I decided, for music's sake, to let my guard down a bit with him. For music's sake, I would give this church a try.

'Do you reckon I could watch the band one day?' I asked him.

'Yes, of course,' he replied enthusiastically. He was delighted.

And so I'd keenly watch the keyboardist, bass player, guitarist and drummer play together. I observed as they worked bits out, got things wrong and tried again. I saw the friendship, their bond . . . their family.

Maybe I could have that one day.

As time went by, I mustered the confidence to edge over to the keyboard before the service to try out notes and chords, and soon, from having gone to church only because I was forced to by Carmen, I had grown to find solace in their music. I even began to sing the songs under my breath in the moments when the congregation sang.

I developed a vibrato in my voice and learned how to play basic chords. I wanted the street cred of my foster brother, Reece, but I also wanted music. Music soon became the route through which I could channel the crap and survive life at Carmen's.

Some time after I asked Nina for a keyboard, she popped over for another visit.

'Ashley, I've got some news for you,' she said, fixing a serious expression on her face. 'I spoke to my manager about you wanting a keyboard. Money is never easy to sign off at the council . . . But she agreed that we can get you your keyboard and piano lessons!'

I could see it pleased her to tell me this and I tried to control the grin that was forcing itself across my pre-teen face.

'Thank you, Nina,' I said in a grateful, childlike tone. Because I *was* grateful. I felt like she cared.

Soon, a Yamaha keyboard was in my bedroom and, day after day, I stumbled over the notes, just like I did in life, until, eventually, I learned to play something sweet. And it wasn't long after getting that keyboard that I found myself playing in bands at both school and church. Music made life worthwhile.

In that first year or so at Carmen's, my mum continued to visit me regularly. But on one occasion, she had a bit of news for me.

As normal, she picked me up from Carmen's to take me out. We had now graduated completely from the supervised visits, and this time, she took me to a water fountain under Tower Bridge. The location had sentimental associations for her; we'd often visit 'personal' spots together, and I always saw that she got a lot out of taking me to places that meant a lot to her.

'I used to come here as a kid,' she said with an air of nostalgia.

Although she was my mum, and although I was the child, she often displayed childlike qualities and vulnerabilities that made me feel like the more responsible one. But still, the world always lifted from my shoulders when I was with my mum. There was a safety and lightness. That was until this point . . .

As we sat near the water fountain. I could see she was teary.

'Honey, I have something to tell you today . . . I have decided to go and live in Manchester, up north.'

She had found a job there, she explained.

I just looked at her. Then I asked, 'Will you come back?'

'Well, I want to stay in touch with you, son – but I'm going to be up there permanently. I want to be there long term.'

I didn't know what to say after that. I just sat there. What about me? The wonder of being at the water fountain with my mum swiftly evaporated in a moment. I was back in the shadows. Back under that cloud of rejection. Abandoned.

I started to cry. This dose of rejection was hard to swallow.

My mum put her arm around me. 'Don't worry, Ashley. I've spoken to Nina and she's gonna find a way for us to stay in touch.'

Just when I thought I'd mastered being let go, I was back to being that little vulnerable boy who was turfed from Joyce's home. Not even my mum wanted to be around me. In fact, she'd now decided to move to another part of the country.

Back then, I never thought about why she may have wanted to leave London; what her reasons were. I never thought about the fact that I lived in the areas where she grew up, where she had also spent time in care. Maybe London reminded her of everything she'd had to endure. Regardless, all I could think about as a kid was the pain of, once again, being let go.

The day quickly ended after that, and I was back at Carmen's. And as unhappy as I was in that home, it occurred to me that Carmen was the only person who would have me. Carmen was the only person who cared to feed me, clothe me and provide a bed for me. That was something.

I didn't tell Carmen anything. She didn't ask me questions. She may have known about my mum's move through Nina, but still, we never spoke about any of it. I knew not to expect that form of compassion. I simply went to my room, hoping for the pain to go away.

When my mum finally made the move to Manchester, she called me regularly and I always felt she still cared. Months into her move, she had found a boyfriend called Harper. She'd tell me about friends she met in her new world and how great things were going with her work in telesales.

Despite being older and being my mum, maybe, just like me, she was also trying to find her home – her place in the world. Maybe she felt the same abandonment that I felt in care. Maybe she was looking for love. Maybe Manchester was her only hope.

When it came to my mum, I always took Joyce's advice. Back in the day, Joyce had told me to always love her and to know that she did her best by me. It was Joyce who had explained to me that my mum had also spent time in care, was treated badly and was a victim of the circumstances she was forced to grow up in. It seemed I was part of a cycle of generational care. Joyce told me that, one day, I would break that cycle.

It was well over a year after my mum had moved out of London that Nina posed an unexpected question.

'Ashley, how would you feel about spending a weekend with your mum in Manchester?'

That stunned me. 'What? Overnight?' I asked in disbelief.

Nina nodded. 'Me and my manager agree it might be a positive step for you to spend a weekend with her.

She's settling in up north really well. She rents a property, is in full-time employment and always asks about you,' she said.

I couldn't believe what I was hearing. I couldn't even stay overnight at a mate's house because that required social services' permission. I'd never slept at my mum's because social services had never allowed that kind of contact between us. So this opportunity to spend a weekend with Mum felt like a dream.

'I would really like to do that,' I said, still in a state of shock.

And just like that – within weeks – Nina was taking me to a central London train station and seeing me off on a train to Manchester.

12

MANCHESTER LIGHTS TO ST LUCIAN WATERS

I sat on the train, peering through the window. As it slowly pulled out of the station, my eyes darted from left to right, taking in the sweeping scenes.

I was a mixture of thrills and anxiety. It was exciting to be on a train and this was the first time – now in my early teens – that I was travelling outside of London alone. I was curious to see where my mum lived. What was Manchester like? I knew she had a boyfriend called Harper. Would I like him? Would he like me?

As the train sped on, I thought about all the possible scenarios of how things might go on that weekend. Maybe if it went well, I could live with her, I thought to myself. Just the permission to spend the weekend with my mum caused my mind to run wild with hopes of what could be.

The journey lasted for a couple of hours or so before I spotted a Manchester Piccadilly Station sign as we edged in alongside a platform. I got off the train with my sports bag. The buzz of people at the station, the train officers giving directions to confused travellers and the sound of the Manchester dialect all stirred an excitement within me.

I heard my mum's voice calling for me as I walked along the train platform. Spotting her, I ran up to her and jumped into her arms like I did at Roseberry Street.

She looked happy to see me. 'Hello, babes,' she said, with full emotion.

Holding my hand, she led me down an escalator and then we jumped into a cab. We slowed up outside an imposing tower block.

'We're here, thanks,' my mum shouted to the driver.

Leaving the cab, I looked up at the towering block which now loomed over me.

'Here we are, son. This is my home.'

We entered the building and took a lift to one of the higher floors. As we went up, I looked at my mum with a grin of excitement. Although we had no plans to do anything specific, my heart was racing. This all felt like an action-packed discovery to me.

Walking into her flat, the pleasant aroma of bubble bath filled my nostrils. We were in a small passageway which led to an open living area with wide windows overlooking a breathtaking view of the Manchester skyline.

It was still daytime but we were nearing sunset. I looked out at the view, wide-eyed.

'That's Old Trafford Stadium – Manchester United's ground,' Mum said, pointing to a luminous red blob in the distance.

'I know Old Trafford is Man U's ground!' I retorted. My light sense of annoyance at my mum's comment made me feel like a normal child.

Soon, the sun began to lower and I watched the city lights flicker, like distant candles, across the skyline through Mum's living room window. I felt light. Being in that flat, observing the Manchester sky, sparked an optimism that I'd rarely felt before; being there gave me a sense of comfort I hadn't always felt under the glare of the social workers who used to supervise my meetings with Mum.

That evening, over a Chinese takeaway, I mustered a bit of courage and asked, abruptly: 'Mum, why did you put me into care?'

I could see my mum was taken aback. I didn't know I had it in me to challenge someone like this.

She breathed heavily. 'Ash, I'm so sorry that I couldn't be there for you . . .' She paused between sentences, treading carefully through every word she uttered. 'I was young when I had you. I was a child.

'I always said to myself that I'd leave you to have your own journey when it comes to your dad, and to let you gain your own views . . .' I could see my mum was pained as she spoke.

'If I could have kept you, I would have, son. But I was too vulnerable to be able to give you the love and support you needed.'

At that point, there was a lot that my mum didn't say about why I was put in care. There was a lot in her story that, at that time, I was too young to understand.

But, ultimately, I knew that she loved me and that she would have done everything she could to have kept me.

She then hugged me which felt like a warm cup of hot chocolate. Since leaving Joyce, hugs were not something I was used to.

That night, I slept on a mattress in Mum's living room. As she turned off all the lights, I looked out at the Manchester skyline one more time. Lights still blazed in the distance. And just as the Manchester horizon loomed through Mum's window, I thought maybe beautiful things stood on the horizon for me, too.

I slept peacefully that night. It was the closest I had ever felt to being a true son. Sleeping under the same roof as my mum, I was connected to her in a way I'd never felt before. She had gained a little weight compared to how she looked in the original photo that Joyce had given me when I was years younger, but still, being with her at home, she was as radiant and angelic as I used to imagine. There was no part of me that blamed her for my childhood. I had an innate trust in who she was and who she was working so hard to become.

Over that weekend, we watched films on DVD, ate out in the local Trafford shopping centre. She told me about her boyfriend, Harper, and explained a bit more about her job in telesales. We laughed so much. But the weekend went all too quickly, and soon, I was on a train back to London and, as ever, dreading the reality of going back to Carmen's.

A couple of years into living with Carmen, the rhythm of my life was well-established, and I had settled for it.

It was a good thing, especially to my social worker, that I had managed to not be excluded. I was surviving at Bacon's College so far, and for all my behavioural issues, I'd been able to make a half-decent reputation for myself through music. My piano skills had developed to the point where I was able to take exams – a source of great pride for me, as well as for the senior teachers. My reputation was split between suspensions and my emerging talent for music.

Mr Tunbridge even chose me to play piano for the school choir when (then) Prince Charles turned up at our school on a visit with some posh, religious guy, apparently known as the Archbishop of Canterbury. I couldn't grasp in that moment that I had played in front of royalty; I was just proud that I'd remembered the chords for the performance.

Alongside school, I had also made inroads in the youth church. The music and community I'd once been so judgemental of had become a bit of a safe space. Tim even occasionally invited me to have dinner with his parents, who he still lived with. Maybe he felt sorry for me. But on the few occasions that I'd eat with them, I'd keenly observe the pleasant and polite exchanges between his parents. To me, they represented a version of family life that I'd perhaps only ever seen on telly. The small, trivial moments seemed significant for them. They valued their time together. They seemed to enjoy the mundane. Maybe I could have a nice and idyllic family like Tim's one day, I thought.

Aside from all this, I had also made some friends in the local area and found a way to cope with the void I still felt all too often at Carmen's. But then, one particular day, Carmen's vibe was completely different.

'Ashley, we have something exciting coming up that we want you to be a part of! Me, Reece and Harvey are going to a studio to take some family photos with a photographer. It would be nice to have some photos with you, too?' she said. It sounded more like a question, but the upbeat tone was rare for Carmen.

Fast forward a few days and that Saturday, we boys were clad in smart shirts and jeans, as Carmen drove us to the photo shoot.

'Mum, this is long, you know,' said Reece.

'This will be good for us, son,' Carmen replied.

Sat between Reece and Harvey in the back of her car, I felt a warm sense of acceptance to have been included in the family shoot. Maybe Carmen was growing to see me as part of her family. Maybe she didn't really see me as a mistake, after all.

We arrived at the studio and entered a room full of lights on stands, stalls and a white backdrop. I looked around. I felt slightly excited. Maybe it was the energy of being in a creative space.

A friendly man with a camera hanging from his neck greeted us. I stood behind Carmen's boys who were much taller than me, peeking up. Carmen deliberated with the man about the shoot. He then gestured to her sons.

'Okay, you two. Can you please stand behind the stool on the set. We'll get your mum to sit on the stool with the two of you standing behind her. That okay?' he said.

They nodded and took their positions. I was politely nudged off to the side from where I looked on. Carmen then sat down in front of her boys, smiling enthusiastically. Proud.

'Oh, come on, lads! Give us a smile!' The man cajoled Reece and Harvey. They both began to laugh with a bit of shyness, and the photographer snapped away on his camera.

'Lovely, fellas . . . bigger smiles!'

I watched Carmen with her sons, all posing and smiling. A perfect family frame. I looked on in amusement. Carmen then nodded for me.

'Hey, pal, wanna come in for some of these photos?' the man said, looking at me.

It may well have been clear to this man that I wasn't really part of the family. Knowing that I stood out made me feel a bit embarrassed. But still, I made my way to the set where the man gestured for me to stand next to Reece and Harvey, behind Carmen.

'All right, boys, I want big smiles, please!'

Maybe something here appealed to the unknown performer in me because I managed to pull off a few smiles.

Snap, snap. A blue light flickered from the man's camera as he took more photos.

Standing next to Reece and Harvey in this setting sparked a belonging. And while I knew I didn't *really* belong, it was at least nice to pretend in the moment. I had never taken a family photo like this before. It was nice to be included.

Before long, the shoot was over and we made our way home. We'd have to wait a few days for the photos to be printed I was told. Deep down, I was a bit excited to see how I looked – how *we* looked.

A few days later, I arrived back from school at Carmen's, threw off my bag and coat and went into the living room. There, on the wall, was a large framed print of one of the photos taken at the shoot over the weekend.

The photo was of Reece, Harvey and Carmen, beaming with joy. I wasn't in it. The photos with me included hadn't made the living room wall. I gazed at the photo. A feeling of sadness hit my gut. I didn't know why.

Carmen appeared behind me. 'Ah, you've seen the photo,' she said lightly.

'It's really good,' I replied.

'Well, that's not the only one I printed out,' she exclaimed, handing me a small key ring with a photo of me, the boys and her.

That felt like a consolation prize for not making the main living-room-wall photo.

'I hope you like it,' she said.

'It's really nice,' I lied.

Carmen then made her way back to the kitchen, and as I sat to watch telly, I couldn't help but stare endlessly at the new, large living room photo in its regal wooden frame. It stood as a reminder that I really didn't belong. I really wasn't part of the family, if I wasn't seen as worthy of being included on the living room wall.

Over the days and weeks to come, regardless of the mood I was in when I entered the living room, that photo would serve me a gut punch, reminding me that I never made the main family photo.

It wasn't the sort of thing that I cried or complained about. But just like the times foster families had let me go, it felt like another moment of unwantedness. Another rejection that I harboured in silence.

I'm not sure why, but as I grew older, random and trivial things triggered deep despair within me. For the most part, I do think I was somewhat happy. Sometimes, though, the smallest thing could set me off.

I would have been around thirteen when, on a winter's evening, Carmen took me to our local supermarket to buy groceries. It was a regular occurrence and, as normal, I walked impatiently alongside Carmen, really wanting to be back at home where I could play the Nintendo.

As we strolled down an aisle, I saw a random man with a little boy, who appeared to be his son. They were playfighting. The boy couldn't have been any older than five. The man lifted the boy up and swung him over his shoulders. The boy started laughing hysterically, with a joy I'd rarely encountered. Though it was just a moment in time, I saw the love between this father and son.

Continuing to walk with Carmen, my heart sank. Seeing that boy made me question my own life. Where was *my* dad? Why didn't I ever have a father figure to play around with – to laugh with? That boy was like a mirror, showing me the family I didn't have.

Carmen and I continued to stroll around the supermarket, as she picked her meat, veg and other bits. All the while, in my mind, all I could see was that boy's smiles and laughter as his dad played with him. Those moments of normality and family were simply foreign to me. At Carmen's I simply got by. Existed from day to day, without a deep sense of identity or connectedness.

I kept my thoughts to myself, but as soon as we arrived back at Carmen's house, I ran to my bedroom, lay face down on my bed and wept. I tried to cry silently, breathing deeply and being as quiet as possible with my sniffles. I wasn't entirely sure why the image of that particular boy had been so upsetting, but I just wished that I could feel like a normal son in a normal family.

Despite regularly attending church, I had never really subscribed to any religious belief. But in that moment on my bed, I remembered the words once uttered in church – that God made people like me with a purpose. I wasn't a mistake. And in my vulnerability, with no one else to cry to, I asked God to be my father.

Perhaps, as I got into my mid-teens, I simply became more self-aware and mindful of what it meant to be a foster kid, but for whatever reason, life at Carmen's continued to spiral. Over time, respite periods had become almost routine, with Carmen frequently requesting two-week breaks, and the harder life got with her, the more I got suspended from school.

One day, as I was sat outside the head teacher's office, awaiting a suspension letter, a history teacher called Ms Lincoln walked over to me. With a look of concern, she said, 'Ashley, you're a bright lad, but if you keep getting called up here for your behaviour . . . well, you're not gonna end up anywhere good. Sort it out.'

But she didn't have a clue about what life was like for me. My future at Bacon's was the least of my worries. In fact, my future more broadly wasn't particularly a priority. I grappled daily with just trying to get by without really having anyone who seemed to truly care about me.

When it came to being at Carmen's, there was an unexplainable chasm – one that only got bigger. Whether it was the major life moment of getting my first proper girlfriend, doing well in something music-related or falling out with a friend, I never shared things with her.

Another development in my life with Carmen was that now, when Reece wasn't around, she no longer ate meals with me in the living room. At some point, she'd started to eat by herself in the kitchen while I ate at the dinner table.

As far as my social worker was concerned, Carmen was great. She ticked all the boxes on their assessment forms: fed me, clothed me, saw me through school. But how could I, a young boy, find the language to communicate that chasm? How could I explain that over time, she'd even begun to see her relatives for Sunday lunch without inviting me? After church, I'd spend Sunday afternoons at home alone. Was that something that I was entitled to be anxious or upset about?

As usual, I just kept it all inside, knowing that Carmen was probably the best option I had as a looked-after child. Honesty wasn't a two-way thing. As the care kid, it was my job to be silent and grateful. She was entitled to her respites, her breaks, but was I entitled to feel rejected and abandoned in those moments? Was my voice of concern to anyone? Hell, no.

My evergreen escape from the pain was music. I'd go to my bedroom and, over basic chords, I'd write lyrics and melodies about how, one day, I'd overcome.

Life carried on at Carmen's, and I remained firm in my belief that she didn't really care about me. But then another development came out of left field, causing me to question my presumptions about her.

One day after school towards the end of the academic year, she approached me in the living room, as I was watching telly.

'Ashley, me and Reece are going on holiday to St Lucia. It's where my mum's from. I've been speaking with Nina and she's agreed to pay for you to come with us.'

I paused. I didn't feel particularly excited. Maybe I should have pretended. If anything, it baffled me. Why did she want me there? We barely spoke and it often felt like she didn't want me around at all. Maybe she felt bad about the respites? Was this her way of easing her guilt?

'Where is St Lucia?' I asked.

'It's in the Caribbean,' Carmen replied.

'Like Jamaica?'

'Yes.'

Joyce was from Jamaica. I wished she had taken me to her country of origin. With Carmen, I felt like I lived in a perpetual state of isolation, under a cloud of rejection, until she threw out the odd generous gesture, like St Lucia. It didn't help me understand where I stood with her. Deep down, these gestures would cause me to hope, yet again, that maybe I did matter to her. It was confusing.

Still, the trip to St Lucia went ahead, and after an eight-and-a-half-hour flight, we were there. The island was beautiful, hot and tropical.

Carmen's elderly mum – who we were staying with – lived on the coast. Arriving at her house, I was nervous. It felt like New York all over again. Would she accept me as part of her family?

I was told to call Carmen's mum, Aunty. Arriving at her door, I plucked up as much courtesy and courage as possible.

'Hello, Aunty,' I said. 'It's nice to meet you.'

'Hello, young man,' she responded.

Her eyes pierced me. It felt like she was examining me. I wonder what she saw . . . She was small in stature but a giant among the local residents in Vieux Fort. People would often come by to drop off food and check in on her. On meeting her, she instantly commanded respect.

After dumping our luggage, I threw on some swimming trunks and went off with Reece to the local beach, as directed by Carmen. As we walked down a hill, locals waved at us. The friendliness of this community was infectious and nothing like I'd ever seen in London.

The bond and power within this community became instantly clear to me, adding further confusion to my impression of Carmen. If this was her heritage, how come she often appeared to be so cold with me? Why didn't she seem, in our relationship, to embody the spirit of the community she came from? I wondered, yet again: did she do it for the money social services gave her for looking after me?

As Reece and I reached the beach, I instantly ran into the sea, where others were also splashing and having fun. The water was translucent. An array of blues, purples and greens swirled around. I even spotted a few tropical fish darting around my feet.

Floating on my back I looked up into the clear sky. A feeling of slight melancholy emerged. As much as I loved that moment, being in the sea, I just wished that I could be a real son. I wished that I didn't have to feel like the third wheel, the addition that wasn't really wanted or welcomed.

Reece soon called for me, and we made our way back to Carmen's mum's house. As with all the homes I'd moved to, I didn't know what awaited me.

Living with Carmen's mum was a culture shock. Used to the smouldering heat, she wasn't big on air con and was clearly accustomed to the mosquitos. We'd be awoken early in the mornings by the roosters and accompanied at night by the chirping of crickets. There was something pleasing about being more embedded in nature here, compared to back in London.

I saw Carmen come alive in St Lucia in a way that I'd never seen in London. She was relaxed and at ease with the locals and would joke with people she met. I could see the deep connection she had with her mother. And while Reece was, at heart, a Londoner, I could see the joy that being on this island of his heritage brought him, too.

But as for me? Well, as much as I tried, yet again, to be part of the family, I couldn't fake it. I couldn't manufacture the deep connection with the island they naturally felt. This wasn't a homecoming for me. I didn't feel like I was having some sort of reunion with a long-lost relative when I was around Carmen's mum.

Observing Carmen's family in their homeland made me wonder about my own background. My mum was white British. My dad was Black. I knew from the life story work I did with social services that he, too, was of Caribbean descent. From Dominica, I think.

During my time in St Lucia, I wondered if I had relatives in Dominica. Maybe a real aunty or two. A beach that was local to my biological relatives. I wondered how my dad's voice sounded. Did he have a Caribbean accent? What did he look like? What was his story of growing up in the Caribbean before moving to the UK?

The more Carmen and Reece settled into holiday life in St Lucia, the more I considered my own Caribbean heritage. I wondered if my dad had ever asked about me. Did he enquire with social services about my where-abouts?

Did he even care? Did I have siblings? My mind ran wild with all the possibilities about my Caribbean family background. Did I come from slaves, perhaps? Truth be told, I had absolutely no connection to my Caribbean heritage and I'd never thought for a moment Nina or social services could help me find out more. If anything, I felt more Jamaican than I did Dominican because of Joyce. I was familiar with the Jamaican cuisine she cooked and I remembered some of her stories about growing up in Kingston. Despite all the years since leaving her, I still thought about her so often. The memory of her was imprinted on my brain more than any other home I had lived in.

So as grateful as I was to be on holiday in St Lucia, it became a painful trigger for my lack of knowledge and awareness around my own identity.

Who was I?

The only thing I could really hold on to was music and the nascent faith I was exploring that told me I wasn't a mistake, despite how I got here.

As ever, I didn't share any of these thoughts with Carmen or Reece. I kept them to myself and feigned as much enjoyment as possible. St Lucia was such a beautiful island. I just wished I was there with the family I never had.

13

A WAY OUT

Time went on and my isolation felt more acute. There was no clear reason as to why, though. My behaviour at Carmen's hadn't deteriorated and my growing passion for music gave me a clear channel through which to harness some of the stuff I felt inside. And while I wasn't excelling at school, at least I was still there. I hadn't been kicked out yet. If anything, I was becoming 'better'. At least, that's how I saw it. But maybe, for Carmen, the cost of looking after me wasn't worth the money she was getting paid.

As Reece was out most of the time, Carmen continued to eat away from me on the smaller kitchen table during dinner time. I spent more and more Sunday afternoons alone, as Carmen would eat lunch at her sister's or some other relative's. Our relationship was purely functional. If she had an instruction for me, or if I needed something, they'd be our only exchanges, and I resigned myself to this existence.

I found an escape with my mates at school. Andre, the drummer, became like a brother (although my fear of rejection would never have allowed me to admit that). Social services allocated a daily amount of money for my school dinners and often I'd have spent the whole lot by the 11am break. Far too often, therefore, I'd find myself going up to Andre and asking him to lend me some cash for food. He never turned me down or embarrassed me in front of the other boys. For years, Andre and one other schoolmate, Carlos, were the only ones to know about me being fostered.

I can still remember the occasions where Andre's dad would take me and his son on trips over the weekend. Once, he took us to a gospel concert with live music, lighting and singers. I never told Andre this, but those moments were safe spaces in the turbulence of my home life. Maybe his dad could sense the rejection I felt.

It was during a bad spell with Carmen that we had another review with the social workers. And yet again, she requested a two-week respite. As previously, the professionals crammed on to Carmen's sofas, drinking tea, and asked why.

'It's just little things,' Carmen said.

'Like what?' probed Nina. She looked mildly frustrated.

'Any time I ask him to wash a cup that he's finished with, well, he just leaves it on the floor next to the sofa or on the table. He just doesn't listen,' Carmen responded.

Carmen's reasoning for wanting the respite admittedly hurt me. I had borne this news before, but on this occasion, I ran to the downstairs bathroom and cried, unable to hold back the tears.

This marked a real turning point at Carmen's. The feeling of being on probation with her, of trying to be accepted, would clearly never go away. I was tired and fed up.

Maybe it was the slight change in Nina's approach with Carmen, or maybe it was the overspill of my emotion, but for some reason, I found my voice during this review. I went back to the living room, puffy-eyed.

'Are you okay, Ashley?' asked Nina.

The reviewing officer and Carmen's social worker, Iris, were also present.

'I just don't get why I keep being thrown away,' I responded in stutters, my voice shaking.

The professionals all chimed in with what I thought to be fake concern.

'Oh no, Ashley. That's not what's happening. Sometimes, foster carers just need a bit of time to rest and bounce back so they can support you properly,' said the reviewing officer.

To me, that sounded bloody patronising. 'Carmen doesn't want to look after me. She doesn't even like me,' I said.

A rush of honesty then spilled out. 'On Sundays, she doesn't take me out for the lunches she goes to with her family. She just leaves me here at home. It's embarrassing to say this, but sometimes I even eat with my youth pastor's family, just so that I don't have to be here alone.

'We don't talk. If Reece is out, she eats in the kitchen and leaves me to eat at the dining table by myself. Only when Reece is around does she come to the table to eat. She can be so cold!

'I just don't know why I'm here in the first place. I was better off back at the children's home.'

I was breathing heavily. Panting. I normally put up a good front. Yet here I was in the aftermath of tears, bright red, with my voice trembling.

Carmen seemed to be fuming. She didn't say anything.

The professionals looked on. I didn't care. Maybe they had pity for me. Or apathy. I didn't really have anything to lose, did I? On paper, Carmen appeared to be a good carer. But in reality, this was a den of isolation, and I was constantly made to feel second class. I was sick of this shit cycle of being let go and being passed on. I would've been better off anywhere else. I was done with trying to be liked, trying to be accepted.

Carmen's social worker, Iris, spoke. She had a sharp, high tone.

'Ashley, for the few years that you've been here, Carmen has only ever been supporti—'

'That's rubbish,' I interrupted, indignant. 'You like to think that. You just tick boxes and believe everything she says. How often do you ask about how I feel?'

Iris sounded like a frustrated teacher about to hand out a detention. 'Ashley, we ask you how things are going every time we have these review meetings. I speak with Carmen regularly. I know first-hand all the good she does to support you!'

I felt like my voice was being quashed.

Nina stepped in. 'I'm sure you see Carmen's efforts, Iris. But Ashley's views, right now, are also valid.'

'That's right, Nina,' said the reviewing officer. Then, 'Ashley – I'm sorry to hear about your concerns. We will have to organise another respite placement for you straight away, as that's Carmen's wish. But I know Nina will speak with you further about the things you've just said. And I'll be sure to catch up with her.'

I remained silent. I suspected I'd no longer be living at Carmen's after the respite. I just wanted to hide away. To escape this roomful of vultures. Everyone around me was on the payroll, except for me. They all got their wages. As usual, I got rejection.

Not long after this, everyone left. I went to my room. Carmen and I didn't exchange a word.

The next day, after school, Nina was waiting for me at the school gate. She took me for some food.

Her approach was nothing like it had been before. She seemed genuinely worried. 'Ashley, it was really concerning hearing you speak last night. Is that really the case, what you said? That she'll often leave you alone at home on Sundays to have lunch with her relatives?'

I nodded.

'I am so sorry. I had no idea.' Nina sounded appalled, and I could see she was upset. 'If I had known, we would have spoken to her. If you don't tell us that stuff, Ashley, it's really hard to know what's going on.

'Now that you've said that, though, a lot makes sense. Well done for speaking up.'

Walking around the local Surrey Quays shopping centre, Nina explained that she'd found me a respite placement with a British Jamaican couple called Eve-lyn and Clinton. They lived in a part of south London called Catford.

'Ashley, I want you to see how the placement goes and maybe take time to reflect on how you feel about Carmen. I am sorry about how you've been feeling.'

Within a matter of days, on a bright spring afternoon, Nina was accompanying me to Evelyn and Clinton's. As ever, I had no idea what to expect.

We arrived at their house on a road lined with white semi-detached houses. Nina rang the doorbell. At this point, anything would have been better than Carmen's, I thought to myself.

I had always found a way to numb the pain of being moved on, but today, I was so desperate for a better foster home. Maybe God would hear my silent prayer.

A short Black woman, with big brown eyes, who looked to be in her forties and clad in a professional suit, answered the door. Her warm voice boomed.

'Hello, Ashley. Welcome!' She bent down and gave me a big hug.

I was nearing fourteen years old at this point, and I couldn't remember the last time someone had hugged me. The feeling of her embrace, even now, is hard to describe. Sensational.

'Lovely to see you, too, Nina.'

'Ashley, this is Evelyn, your respite carer,' Nina said, after Evelyn finally let me go.

I looked at Evelyn. She looked back with twinkling eyes and a glistening smile. 'Hello, Evelyn. Thanks for taking me in,' I replied.

'It's my pleasure. Come on in now.'

Evelyn ushered us inside. A natural warmth and vanilla scent filled her hallway. Instinctively, my hunched shoulders dropped. Relief.

As a looked-after child, you develop a sixth sense when it comes to acceptance, home and the feeling of being welcome. I instantly knew I was in a better place here than at Carmen's.

'Clinton, my partner, and now your foster dad, is at work. My daughter, Kelly, is still at school. You'll see them all later today, love.'

Evelyn showed us her 'guest' living room. Spotless white walls, magnolia sofas and draped curtains, with vases of flowers placed around the room. Then there was another, where the family congregated to watch telly. The open kitchen and living space were furnished with a dining table and ornaments. The place felt massive but intimate at the same time.

Nina followed behind. No doubt, she would have been noting my reactions.

Family photos were dotted around the house. Evelyn pointed at one. 'Those are my daughters, Kelly and Diane. Kelly is in the same school year as you. Diane has her own place with my grandson, Kyan. Everyone is excited to meet you!'

Evelyn seemed to lavish words of affirmation and a warm welcome on me. The attention in the context of a foster home felt foreign but nice.

'Do you want to see your bedroom, Ashley?' Evelyn asked fondly.

I nodded. Walking up the stairs, I couldn't believe that I'd just been catapulted here. Carmen already seemed so far behind me.

Evelyn's house had four bedrooms. She walked to one door and opened it, motioning for me to walk in.

A single bed, with dark blue bed sheets. A number of clean towels were on a chest of drawers. There were also a bunch of new, clean boxer shorts and socks, still in the packaging.

'I hope it's okay, Ashley. I thought I'd get you some underwear, just in case. Your luggage can go in the cabinet and drawers. Please let me know if you need anything.'

'Evelyn, it's lovely. Thank you,' Nina chimed in.

'Yes. Cheers, Evelyn. It's cool,' I said.

'Lovely,' Evelyn chirped.

Nina eventually left, and I sat in the kitchen as Evelyn moved around doing bits and pieces. She then walked over to me.

'Ashley, for the next two weeks, this is your home. Make yourself feel at home. You're welcome. I know it can't be easy, but I really hope that you'll feel comfortable soon enough.'

Evelyn had a natural authority and kindness about her. When she spoke to me, her eyes pierced me, as if she could read my soul.

Within a couple of hours, Kelly was home from school. I straightened up as I heard a key in the front door lock.

'Relax, Ashley,' Evelyn said to me, as if sensing my sudden angst.

'Hi, Mum,' called Kelly. She walked into the kitchen area, casually taking her earphones out.

'Oh, yeah! Today's the day Ashley arrives!' she said, looking at me.

I smiled nervously.

'Hello, Ashley. I'm Kelly!'

'Hi,' I said.

Her natural ease and confidence dominated the room. She was pretty and bubbly.

Her dad, Clinton, soon followed. 'Ashley, young man. Welcome!' he said, patting my shoulder.

'Hello, Clinton.'

This felt like a welcome parade. I sat on the corner of their kitchen sofa, watching as Evelyn, Clinton and Kelly buzzed around the kitchen, chatting and getting dinner ready.

And then the doorbell rang.

'Kelly, that's Diane and Kyan. Let them in, please.'

Moments later, Evelyn's other daughter and her son, four-year-old Kyan, were also in the room.

'Diane, make Ashley welcome, please,' said Evelyn, while busying herself over the cooker.

'Awww, hello!' Diane said, while Kyan gave me a high five, as a slight grin slipped across my face.

Evelyn then began to fill the dinner table with an array of scrumptious food. Curried chicken, white rice, salad, macaroni and cheese. My mouth watered.

'Ashley, come and have a seat here, love.'

I took my place.

Kyan ran around the kitchen with screams of excitement. Kelly urged him to calm down as everyone sat around the dining table. My heart was beating with nerves. I'd been shunted, yet again, into a new home, with a new clan of people, and was now seated at their dinner table. That despairing feeling of being an imposter kicked in once more. I was invading their family. It was all too much.

Evelyn grabbed my hand once the family had all sat down. 'Let's pray,' she said warmly.

Everyone went quiet.

'Father, thank you for our family. Thank you for this meal and thank you for bringing Ashley to us. We are so glad to have him with us.'

Everyone said 'amen' in unison.

My heart fluttered in endearment. A swell of peace. A thread of belonging.

'Now, Ashley. I know you're new,' Evelyn said, looking at me with a grin, 'but I don't care. It took me ages to prepare this good, good food. So, you'd better enjoy it, yes?'

I looked at Clinton. He winked at me. There was silence and then an eruption of laughter.

'Mum, he doesn't get your humour yet!' Kelly piped up, laughing. 'Ashley, she's being silly.'

'I'm not gonna lie, Evelyn. I'm hungry, this looks good,' I said, smiling.

The sounds of clanging cutlery and chatter filled the room. The meal was delicious. It had been a while since I'd had company at a dining table. It felt nice.

Soon after dinner, Diane and Kyan went home, Kelly retired to her bedroom to do homework and I was shown to mine.

Lying on my bed, I felt full both physically and emotionally. Maybe it was possible for a looked-after child to feel accepted in their foster home?

I went to bed happy for the first time in ages.

I think Nina placed me at Evelyn's, at least in part, to maintain continuity on the spiritual front.

Evelyn was a Christian and also invited me to go to church with her and the family. She didn't go to an established denominational church. She explained that it was held in a local school hall and was big on gospel music.

Evelyn's Sunday best consisted of, simply, a nice dress. No Salvation Army uniform or the like. Kelly wore trainers, Clinton a shirt and jeans, and I was told I could wear whatever I wanted. Relief.

As we arrived outside the school hall, Evelyn and the family were showered with welcomes and hugs from other churchgoers.

Whereas Carmen was one of the few Black people at her church, here the majority of people were Black. Young guys turned up wearing snap-back baseball caps, tracksuits and trainers. It was disarming.

Evelyn and Clinton introduced me to a swarm of people. 'This is our new foster son, Ashley,' they said with fondness. I was showered with affection outside that makeshift church, and when we finally entered the school hall, the music was already under way.

A line of trendy-looking singers was supported by the most incredible band I'd ever heard. Tight drumbeats, jazzy gospel chords and basslines with the most amazing vocals and harmonies. As we took our seats, I was awe-struck by the sounds being produced. They were both heartfelt and soulful.

The music moved from upbeat to slower and more emotive. People occasionally shouted out. Others were dancing. I looked over to Evelyn who was deep in the rhythm and worship. This space was undoubtedly filled with love.

Then the music subsided, and after a cheer and applause, people took their seats. The pastor, a towering and friendly-looking man called Denis, took to the podium. His bellowing voice filled the hall.

'If anyone is new here, we'd love to welcome you. All are accepted here. If you feel comfortable, please stand up.'

There was no way on earth I'd be getting up. That was until the whole of Evelyn's clan started tugging at my clothes. I was reluctant and remained silent, not wanting to draw attention to myself. But Evelyn then pointed at me frantically with the aim of catching the pastor's attention.

'Can we please give a special welcome to Evelyn's foster son, Ashley? He's staying with the family for a short while,' said the pastor.

The room erupted with applause.

'Amen! Welcome, brother. Welcome,' people shouted.

I wanted the room to swallow me up. Evelyn rubbed my back. I wasn't used to this sort of love and affection. I didn't know how to receive it, how to react. There was a community spirit here, one of acceptance, that certainly had something heavenly about it.

Afterwards, we made our way home, where Evelyn made an incredible Sunday lunch with all the Caribbean trimmings.

I thought back to the solitary Sunday afternoons and dinners at Carmen's. All of this was anything but. Evelyn seemed to be the sort of person who'd probably take offence if anyone was excluded or left on the margins.

Although I had only been here a couple of days, I already felt an innate sense of acceptance and welcome that Carmen had never seemed to offer. The only shame was that I would have just two weeks at Evelyn's. And so, as much as I settled in, I knew I had to prepare myself for yet another goodbye. Imminently.

That evening, Evelyn ensured that I had everything ready for school. 'Do you have any homework to do?' she asked.

Carmen never asked this question and it wasn't something I took seriously. No one seemed to care about it, so why should I?

'Er, yeah, I think so,' I replied.

'Think so? Do you have a school planner?' she asked, bemused.

'Yeah. Don't really use it, though.'

'Okay, Ashley. Well, while you're here, you're going to have to do your homework. Just like Kelly. From tomorrow, I want to see your school planner and I want you to make a note of all the homework you have across all your subjects. Are we clear?'

I nodded.

She had Myles vibes. And for me, at fourteen, this was the part of her that I found irritating.

Evelyn was caught up on all sorts of details that no one had ever pulled me up on: 'Have you ironed your trousers for school?' 'Is everything packed for the morning?' She was almost militant in making sure I was ready for the school week. Maybe this was what they called tough love?

The next morning, Clinton, a painter and decorator, was busy packing his car with his work equipment. Evelyn was getting ready for work and Kelly was running between mirrors, ensuring her image was spot on.

The morning rush had an energy that was appealing. Though everyone was doing their own thing, there was a sense of teamwork and all doing their bit to contribute to the wider mechanics of family. Maybe they were unaware of it, but I could see the love and unity amid all their separate and collective frantic activity.

After goodbyes, I drove off with Clinton. He was the first foster dad I'd ever had, and although Evelyn was the proactive and more vocal one, taking the lead in caring for me, when travelling with Clinton in the mornings, I got to know him better.

Clinton was an Arsenal fan. He liked going to the pub every Friday. He seemed to love his family deeply. He lived with a simplicity that taught me a lot during those weeks. He put his family first. And it didn't take long for me to observe and understand these things.

The two weeks flew by and as my respite drew to an end, a feeling of despair bubbled up inside. The thought of moving back to Carmen's began to stifle my ability to do anything. Once again, I was being shown how unfair this care system was.

As I was getting ready for bed one night, there was a knock on my bedroom door.

'Come in,' I said.

Evelyn appeared, wearing her headscarf and dressing gown. 'Ashley,' she said, 'if you don't mind, I'd like to know how you've found it living here over the last couple of weeks.' She looked at me with a gentle focus that told me she truly valued what I was about to say.

'I really like your home and family, Evelyn. Everyone's been really nice. Thank you for taking me in and looking after me.' It pained me to think that I would very shortly be leaving.

Evelyn smiled. 'And how have things been for you with Carmen?'

I had a feeling she already had a sense of how things had been going. Still, I was honest. 'I don't think Carmen really likes having me live with her. Maybe she does it for the money. I am really going to miss you, Evelyn,' I said, feeling both vulnerable, yet safe.

As authoritative as she was, Evelyn appeared delicate in this moment, looking at me from the bedroom door. 'Ashley. I've been thinking . . . I've also had a chat with Clinton and Kelly about you. I know that we've only spent two weeks together, but we all have loved having you live here.

'You may not know, but as a family, we are new to fostering. You are our first foster child. Anyway, what I really want to say is that um . . . well . . . if you wanted to live here permanently, we would be delighted to have you as our foster son.'

A flush of emotion filled me and I tried to suppress it. Also disbelief. I looked at her as if to say, 'Really?'

She smiled with a most reassuring nod.

But before I had a chance to give an answer, she spoke again. 'Ashley, you don't have to give me an answer now. Go back to Carmen's, see how you feel and take a week or so to think about it. It's right that you take the time to think it through.'

'Okay,' I said, though truth be told, I would've said yes there and then. There was no part of me that wanted to go back to Carmen's. It was as if Evelyn's words had freed me from an incarceration.

For the first time, a respite requested by Carmen turned out to be in my favour. At this point, I could only thank her for what I deemed to be her act of neglect towards me.

When the time came, Nina arrived to take me back to Carmen's. It was a melancholic goodbye, but I knew it would only be temporary.

Driving back with Nina to Carmen's, my heart plummeted. I still had to do time there. Go back to the silence. The chasm. The isolation.

'Ashley, how was it, then?'

'I really liked living there,' I said with a bit of a smile.

Though driving, Nina gave me a quick, warm glance. 'I am so glad for you, Ashley. And Evelyn's informed me of her offer to foster you permanently. How would you feel about that?'

'Yes, I really want to move there, please.'

'Well, I'll have to organise a meeting with Carmen, yourself and the reviewing officer, so give me a few days, okay?'

Back at Carmen's the two of us exchanged short greetings. When a placement breaks down, it can feel impossible to rebuild it. And here, back in her living room, that sense of coldness once again engulfed me.

She had cooked a lovely meal, but she had already eaten. So sitting alone at the dining table, I tried to think positive thoughts of Evelyn and Clinton.

Now that I knew I had an escape route from Carmen's, a growing indignance arose within me. All of a sudden, I wanted to tell her how much I hated living with her. I wanted her to understand the neglect and abandonment I'd felt all those times she left me at home on Sundays, or failed to include me in family conversations or in the living room family photo.

Maybe she was oblivious to it all. Unaware of the icy pain that can take hold when, as a child, you feel overlooked and forgotten. But I wanted her to know that true 'caring' wasn't just about buying the groceries and making sure I went to the dentist regularly; it was about showing genuine love and inclusion. It was about doing the emotional work of making me feel part of the family. It was about sticking it out and not just fobbing me off to respites when she couldn't hack it.

I wanted her to understand that, like her sons, I had feelings and sensitivities, too. I wasn't a charity case. I wasn't just the beneficiary of her good Christian deeds. I was a human being. And one day, I thought to myself, I would show her.

I didn't say any of this to her. But just by virtue of Evelyn's invite to live with her, I was developing a new sense of self-worth.

Before long, the time had come for the meeting to break the news. As with review meetings, Nina, Iris (Carmen's social worker) and the reviewing officer were all present.

Knowing what I had to say, my heart began to race. I couldn't make eye contact with Carmen. Did she know what was coming?

The reviewing officer kicked things off promptly.

'Ashley, I hear you had a good respite with carers Evelyn and Clinton.'

'Yes, thank you,' I said sheepishly.

Nina then chimed in. 'Yes, there has been positive feedback about the respite from both parties. And why I've called this meeting today is to inform you all – and you, in particular, Carmen – that the family have given Ashley the option to live with them permanently if he wishes to do so.'

My chest tightened. Just hearing Nina say these words triggered a feeling of guilt.

'So, with that said – Ashley, where do you stand?' Nina said to me gently.

Despite everything, I felt guilty for what I was about to say, as if I was dishing out that same blow of rejection that was so often served to me.

I quickly glanced at Carmen. For once she was looking at me. Fiercely, I thought. She didn't blink. Maybe I misinterpreted her look. Maybe she was concerned? Maybe she didn't want me to go. I don't know, but I was bricking it.

I tried to find the courage to speak. My voice was trembling. I was shaking. 'I'm really sorry, everyone. I want to live with Evelyn and Clinton. Sorry, Carmen.'

Silence.

I'd done it. I'd spoken my truth. Yet despite the coldness, the sense of abandonment, the respites, I still felt bad for wanting to live somewhere else.

Carmen displayed a vulnerability that I'd never seen before. 'That's okay, Ashley. That's fine.' Her words were few. She muttered them quietly. Maybe she was feeling the embarrassment I often felt. Maybe she didn't care.

Nina stepped in again.

'Ashley, do you want to thank Carmen?'

'Carmen, thank you for taking me into your home and for being my foster carer. Thanks for everything.' This was the most awkward and uncomfortable break-up, but I knew I had to do it.

Carmen's social worker didn't say anything. The reviewing officer tried to bring things to a formal end. 'Ashley, I am really glad that you've made a decision that you believe will work best for you. Carmen, thank you so much for everything. We will sort out the arrangements for Ashley to move right away. I think we've come to the right outcome for everyone.'

Once I'd gotten over the initial awkwardness of speaking out, my heart settled and a peace took over. I knew I had made the right decision.

Over those last few days at Carmen's, we still didn't talk much. Reece showed some signs of disappointment, but he was far more preoccupied with his social life.

As much as I'd struggled at Carmen's, I developed a mild sympathy for her as the day for me to leave approached. Maybe her inability to show me affection was rooted in her own insecurity as a foster mum – or a regular mum. And if she did it for the money, well, that was another reason to pity her. Whatever drove Carmen, however, I no longer had to worry about it. My time to move on had finally come.

14

WANTED?

I can't recall when I first moved to live with Joyce. She seemed to be there from the beginning, ever since I can remember. With that in mind, the move to Evelyn and Clinton's felt worlds apart from all the other moves that I could remember. Maybe that's because this was the first home where, from the very start, I felt wanted.

As Nina and I drove up to their door, I didn't feel the trepidation and despair that I normally felt during these upheavals. Evelyn wasn't putting me on trial to see if I was good enough. She knew my history and still, she wanted me. She and her family, the Bennetts, were taking me in. Flaws and all.

Moving to theirs from Carmen's was seamless. The family awaited me with open arms, metaphorically speaking. There were questions about my wellbeing and humorous comments. They had prepared a warm meal that felt like it was made with love. And as normal as this stuff might've been to other people, these were the trappings of family that I'd lived without for a very long time.

During those first few weeks of living there officially, I could see that Evelyn was a busy and 'important' person. She worked for the local council and seemed to have an air of authority when it came to her work. In a smart suit and heels, with neat hair and pearl earrings, she trotted around with a handbag and laptop. Whenever she came home in the evenings, though, warmth filled her home. She was alert and present to the everyday moments and always seemed to care.

Clinton's work took him all around London, so he'd never know where he'd be working on any given week. And every evening, Kelly would diligently do her homework. She was clever and did well at school, something that gave Evelyn and Clinton great pride.

But despite the pressures everyone faced in their outside worlds, at home, they merged in harmony. Their varying schedules and priorities would somehow mesh every evening to create a rich sense of family, purpose and belonging.

One thing Clinton couldn't miss after a day's work was the evening news. As Evelyn prepared food in sizzling pots and pans, he'd sit on the sofa in the open kitchen space, crossed-legged, listening to the reporters and their stories on telly. From politics to sports, he'd be outspoken on every issue. A lot of what he said went over my head. But there was something compelling in the way he seemed to be informed and engaged with stuff in the outside world.

As normal as their day-to-day life was for them, to me, it was a spectacle. Every evening at the dinner table they'd ask each other questions, have petty disagreements and general conversation. They were interested in each other. They cared. And whatever the topic – someone was always sure to include me.

It was so different from Carmen's. Here, there was no silence. No chasm. The moments of home life that I once hadn't cared about or had overlooked, I now looked forward to. Being in the Bennetts' home brought a lightness and giddiness that I'd not felt before.

Whenever I moved to a new home, it affected every part of my life. This occasion was no different, as it also meant leaving the church Carmen had made me go to. And, to be honest, as much as I'd initially hated the place, there were people from the youth church I'd grown to like. I would miss them and I'd miss the music.

But Evelyn's church really did make up for that.

On a crisp Sunday morning, we arrived at the school where the church service was held. I walked in sheepishly with the family, and a soulful sound greeted us as we walked along the pews to our seats. The band and singers kicked off with a gospel number. I watched the pianist intently. I took in the chords; they were jazz-like interpretations that amazed me. How did they learn to play like that? The band were tight and appeared to be having the time of their lives. It all sounded, and felt, homely.

As the congregation sang to the music during the service, Evelyn cast an eye on me, bending down to speak in my ear. 'They're good, aren't they, Ashley?' she said, referring to the band.

I nodded enthusiastically.

'Do you want me to introduce you to them after?'

I gave another keen nod.

The service finished and the band began packing away their instruments. Evelyn grabbed my hand and walked me on to the platform to meet some of the musicians.

'Khalid, can I have a word?' Evelyn called out with her typical smile.

The man who had been playing the guitar walked over to us.

'This is my foster son, Ashley. He plays the keyboard really well. Do you reckon you and the band could show him the ropes?'

'Of course, Aunty Evelyn!' Khalid beamed with his friendly face. 'We need more players,' he continued. 'Some of the guys are getting touring gigs with pop stars. We need more reliable players.'

I pulsated with excitement. The band was made up of lads who appeared to be in their twenties. As a group, I instantly looked up to them.

Khalid addressed me directly. 'Here's the deal, Ashley. We often rehearse on Friday nights. You should come if Evelyn will let you! But how about we get you to play a second keyboard next Sunday? That way we can see what you're made of.'

'That would be incredible, mate,' I spluttered in excitement.

'All right, bro. See you next Sunday. Respect.' He gave me a fist bump and went back to packing away his equipment.

I walked off with Evelyn in sheer delight. I had been invited to play next Sunday! I couldn't believe it.

As we drove back home with the rest of the family in the car, everyone bigged me up.

'Yes, Ash. That's wicked,' Kelly commented.

When we arrived home, Evelyn brought out the chicken she'd prepared that morning before church. It was accompanied by bowls of rice, macaroni, seasoned salad and other mouth-watering dishes. The smell of home cooking permeated the house.

Evelyn's other daughter, Diane, soon arrived with Kyan. Sunday lunch was on! As we sat around the table in chatter and laughter, I felt at home. The lonely Sunday afternoons at Carmen's were far behind me. And if anything, those lonesome times made me even more grateful for these Sundays at Evelyn and Clinton's. They were full of love, laughter and belonging.

I stayed on at Bacon's when I moved to Evelyn's. I told Andre about the move, but no one else at school.

Where I had previously got the 381 bus to school from where I lived in Peckham, I now got a train from New Cross.

'We've moved into a massive new house in Catford,' I'd lie to anyone who asked me why I no longer lived in Peckham.

As I edged towards fifteen years of age, the shame of being a looked-after child worsened. I dreaded parents' evenings, and now, I'd have to think up a plausible story to explain who Evelyn and Clinton were.

I'm not even sure if all my teachers knew I was fostered. I often wondered if they were trained to deal with people like me – to be aware of the insecurities and challenges we faced daily as looked-after children.

Over time, life at the Bennetts began to affect life at school. I began to attempt pieces of homework. I'd even try and prepare for exams. Although I was fairly able at school, I'd often get distracted, but even on the occasions when I got in trouble, my work never suffered drastically. If anything, I just got bored. But now, I decided to try and be more intentional. I no longer wanted my disruptive behaviour to overshadow any of my academic potential.

Seeing how seriously Kelly took her schoolwork, on some level, made me want to be better.

Until moving to Evelyn's I hadn't spent a lot of time thinking about my future. I didn't think about jobs or universities or having a family of my own. When you live with the daily insecurity of not knowing when you'll be rejected by a foster family, you don't have the luxury to think about your future. Day to day, I mainly grappled with the immediacy of survival – of trying to stay put in the home I lived in.

Yet as I settled into life with the Bennetts, my performance at school began to matter. Maybe my future *was* important. Maybe I *did* have potential, like Kelly. At least, that was until one day, when I received a few days' suspension for calling a teacher a 'cunt'.

I still remember dreading the reaction of Evelyn and Clinton. Despite the improvements I was making at school, despite the acceptance I felt in their home, I still struggled from time to time with my behaviour. And the suspension, I told myself, would see them kicking me out of their home. Or maybe, like Carmen, they would not respond and just give me the silent treatment.

Having received notice of the suspension, I left school and made my way home, ready for their condemnation. I made my way through the front door and saw Evelyn sat on a sofa, awaiting my return. She didn't look happy.

'So you've been suspended.' It was more a statement than a question.

'I'm sorry, Evelyn, I didn't mean to.'

Looking me square in the face, her eyes filled with care, she stood up and walked over to me.

'Ashley, I know there's been a massive improvement in your behaviour at school. And this incident is NOT who you are. You're better than this. I believe in you. Make sure this doesn't happen again, okay?' Then she smiled at me and walked off.

I couldn't believe her reaction. She still liked me. Still cared.

After the pep talk, I went to my bedroom to play my keyboard. I'll do better, I told myself. I'll show Evelyn that I can do better.

With the move to Evelyn and Clinton's came a new social worker. It was a bit of a sad affair to see Nina move on, to be fair. A lot of the foster kids I knew had a wholly bad view of social services, but Nina proved there were good 'uns and I knew she cared.

Helena, the new one, was a British–Caribbean woman who specialised in seeing older teenagers transition into leaving care. She had a bubbly demeanour and seemed to get on with Evelyn. I was as untrusting as ever, though. I knew better than to take people at face value. I easily could have been one of dozens of kids she was responsible for and didn't assume I'd be a priority for her.

It wasn't too long after meeting her that she made a shock announcement.

'Nina explained that things were going well with you spending time with your mother in Manchester?' Helena probed.

'Yeah, it's all good.'

'I know this doesn't come as a surprise, Ashley, but you know that you won't be a foster child for ever. And having bonds with family beyond care, when possible, is really important.' Helena's spiel wasn't really making much sense to me, but I nodded politely.

'With that, Ashley, I thought it might be nice for you to spend the Christmas holiday with Mum?'

Pause. My jaw dropped. 'What – in Manchester?' I asked.

'Yes, of course! What do you think?' she asked chirpily.

'Yes, that would be cool! Is Evelyn okay with that?' I asked.

'Yeah, she's really supportive. Although she also said she'd love to have you around for Christmas if that's what you'd prefer.'

I was bamboozled. For the first time in my life I had options. Numerous people were interested in me and wanted to be with me over Christmas. This gave me a sense of affirmation that I'd rarely felt in care. I was wanted.

I knew Christmas with the Bennetts would be a good vibe, but I also knew this might be the only opportunity to have Christmas with my mum.

So not long after that meeting, I exchanged fond goodbyes with the Bennetts and made my way up to Manchester on the train.

I thought about sitting with my mum in her flat. Looking at the Manchester lights in the distance from her living room window. We'd watch films, get take-aways, visit spots in Manchester. Just me and Mum. I couldn't wait.

As previously, Mum was waiting for me at Piccadilly Station. I could see the excitement in her eyes, glistening with emotion and tears.

We got to her flat, and that warm feeling of home hit me. It was a place where I felt comfortable. She had put up a Christmas tree and decorated it with an array of different-coloured baubles and Christmas lights, while tinsel lined the edges of the living room ceiling and a pile of presents sat beneath the tree.

She cooked a curry, and we watched telly together. This was a simple pleasure I was grateful for. For the first time in my life, I had my mum to myself for Christmas. That was the best present I could ever hope for.

In bed, later that evening, I wondered how my mum had spent Christmas for all those years we were apart. She had a lot of friends, but who had she spent Christmas day with? Maybe, like me, she knew what it was like to feel alone.

The next day was Christmas eve. Mum cooked us a full English with a drink of Coca-Cola. Mum loved Coca-Cola. She had bought a few bottles for the Christmas season and placed boxes of Quality Street and Celebrations chocolates around the living room, too. I knew my mum had gone to a lot of effort with all these touches.

Late afternoon, Mum took me to Manchester's city centre. It was already dark. Christmas lights lined the streets.

We passed a music store with a grand piano. 'Mum, can I go in?' I begged.

And in we went. Taking a seat at the piano, as last-minute shoppers scurried around the store, I played a few chords in an attempt to impress her, then looked up at her, keen for a response.

'That's so good, babe,' she said, smiling.

During the years I'd spent with Carmen I hadn't got much affirmation for my music, but I took pride in playing what I could in that city-centre shop. Maybe one day, I would go on to make Mum proud somehow.

After a short tram ride, we were back at Mum's flat. The warmth of her home welcomed us as we walked in.

'Mum, can we get Chinese tonight?' I asked, not thinking that she might have prepared food (not to mention it being the evening before Christmas).

'Not tonight, babe. I've already spent a fortune . . .' she said with a note of frustration and tiredness.

'Yeah, but Evelyn sometimes gets me Chinese,' I retorted with a bite of contention.

My words overstepped the mark for Mum. On some level, they triggered her. 'Well then, get the night coach back to London and spend Christmas with Evelyn!' she snapped, then stormed out of the living room.

I went silent. A looming sense of panic filled my belly. Did she really want me to go back to Evelyn's? I never meant to hurt her, yet I knew I had.

Moments later, she came back into the room. Tears were falling down her cheeks. The vibe had turned quickly.

'Sorry, Ash. Of course I don't want you to go back to London. I just know I can't give you everything Evelyn does,' she cried.

I felt guilty for bringing up Evelyn. And for asking for a takeaway. I felt terrible for not considering how sensitive my mum might be feeling over these couple of days of Christmas.

Once I saw how upset she was, it was as if I could sense the pressure she had put herself under. Pressure to make Christmas perfect for me. Pressure to be a good enough mum. Pressure to put on all the bells and whistles of Christmas for her excited son.

Yet there I was, oblivious to the anxiety she was carrying, making a fleeting comparison to Evelyn.

'I'm sorry, Mum. I never meant to bring up Evelyn in that way. Don't worry about getting me takeaway. Sorry.'

This was the first serious moment of tension I'd ever had with my mum.

As Christmas day dawned, I was mindful to show gratitude for every present, for every effort and every plate of food.

She never said it, but for the first time, I could plainly see the huge amount of guilt Mum shouldered when it came to me. For her, Christmas seemed to be an attempt to redeem herself – to make up for lost time.

As a result, even if I was full up, I'd finish every morsel of food. Even if something wasn't to my liking, I'd pretend to be overwhelmingly satisfied and happy. I did whatever it took to convince my mum she was doing a great job and being an incredible mum. I was prepared to exaggerate how happy and content I was with every little thing if it meant my mum felt validated.

Mustering up this sort of emotional vigilance was something I was used to, despite being so young. Moving homes, assimilating into new communities and families produced in me a sensitivity and awareness to people and environments that couldn't be taught or conferred.

It was a gift born of the adversities and rejection I had experienced in the care system.

As my time with Mum over the Christmas period continued, my heightened awareness to her emotional state increasingly overshadowed everything else. It was no longer about the presents or the films. It was no longer about me being the child. I was now the one with the duty of care. I was the one jumping through hoops to accommodate my mum's need for affirmation and approval.

Seeing my mum host Christmas exposed me to a vulnerability in her that I'd never seen so clearly before. And while I loved spending time with her, that Christmas marked a shift. I now realised that she was probably just as needy as I ever was. And, as a result, she didn't seem to have the capacity to be the mum I'd hoped for. Maybe she was just as flawed, imperfect and in need of love as I was. Emotionally, maybe she needed as much from me as I wanted from her. This would be a mother-son relationship like no other.

As I made my way back to Evelyn and Clinton's, I knew I'd miss my mum but I was grateful to be going home, too – where I could be a child.

Back in London, life at Evelyn and Clinton's continued to go well, and I still felt a part of the family in a way that I never had in previous homes. Although one Saturday afternoon, Evelyn's four-year-old grandson's curiosity was sparked: 'Ashley, you're not a part of this family, are you?' he asked innocently. 'Evelyn is not your real mummy.'

Everyone in the room burst out in laughter. Talk about kids telling it like it is!

'Kyan, I am not his mummy like Diane is yours; but Ashley will always be family to us,' Evelyn laughed affectionately.

Evelyn and Clinton were constant in affirming my place in their home and giving me a sense of belonging. Many foster kids wonder if their foster parents look after them just for the money. I'd wondered that myself many times with Carmen. But never with Evelyn and Clinton. They were slowly taking Joyce's place in that I began to hope – and believe – they'd be my forever family.

15

LIFE PREP

Being fifteen sparked new pressures in both school and with the social workers. And despite that hope – that I would stay with Evelyn and Clinton for ever – Helena (the social worker) made it her business to drill into me the fact that I would have to leave care once I turned eighteen.

'Ashley, you should know by now that when you reach the age of eighteen you leave foster care, which means you'll leave this home and will likely move into a council flat.' Helena was very matter-of-fact. This clearly wasn't her first time breaking news like this to foster kids.

This lecture came during my first proper review meeting since I'd moved in with the Bennetts. Evelyn and Clinton hosted the usual group of review professionals in their guest living room.

The reviewing officer spoke after Helena. 'Now that you're fifteen, we need to start preparing you for the realities of leaving care. You'll need to be able to cook for yourself, handle money and bills, maintain your accommodation . . .'

The reviewing officer's speech was anxiety-inducing for me. The prospect of leaving care wasn't something I really thought about. The pressure of survival dominated everything. In many ways, I still felt like the little boy being let go by Joyce. I was still drifting. Still looking for love. Still trying to make sense of this brutal system.

There was no way I'd be able to live alone in three years, I thought to myself. I looked across the room – at the social workers, the reviewing officer and at Evelyn and Clinton. A sober look was plastered on each of their faces. I could see from their expressions that I had some growing up to do.

The review, in some way, marked the end of my honeymoon period at Evelyn and Clinton's. No matter how accepted I felt, or how much I flourished in their home, everything was now underpinned with the awareness that I'd have to leave at eighteen. This could never be my forever family. They too had an expiry date.

Similarly, at school, the pressures of looming GCSE examinations saw the teachers carry a heightened seriousness and intolerance to mischief. Like the prospect of leaving care, this was anxiety-inducing.

I wonder if my teachers understood the crap I was facing. Yes, I had to deal with the normal stuff in terms of exams and thinking about life after school; but did they appreciate the weight I carried in having to prepare for living alone at eighteen while also thinking about GCSEs? It wasn't fair. The combined pressure was isolating. No one I knew could relate.

It was during those weeks when school was hammering home the importance of our GCSEs that I was asked to be seen by the headmaster, Mr Perry. I entered his office and he sat at his desk, looking at me. With grey hair and an arching back, he also carried a natural authority. I didn't particularly get on with him, and as I took a seat, I couldn't help feeling mildly intimidated by the serious look on his face.

'Ashley, are you aware of just how serious your upcoming examinations are for your future prospects?'

At fifteen, I still had a natural disregard for and distrust of authority. 'Obviously. You lot keep banging on about it,' I said dismissively.

'Well, as we gear up to prepare years ten and eleven for their exams, it is important for me to give you a formal caution, given how many times you have been suspended throughout your years at Bacon's.' He didn't flinch while delivering his warning.

I didn't understand what he was saying. 'What do you mean, sir?' I said.

'I mean that if you are issued with another suspension, I'll have no choice but to permanently exclude you,' he said bluntly.

On hearing those words, I felt like the little boy living with Joyce, who had just been excluded from Falondale Primary School.

'But sir, I haven't done anything this time!' I retorted.

'That's true. But Ashley, it's important that students like you, who have been suspended on multiple occasions, understand what's at stake here. The next year or so is critical. We can't have anything or anyone jeopard-ise things for the rest of the students.'

I felt like I was being judged on a former version of who I was and I didn't like it. Hadn't Mr Perry noticed the effort I was making since living with Evelyn and Clinton? Couldn't he see my genuine fear of getting things wrong and being let go by the Bennetts? Didn't he realise that I had more at stake than just GCSEs? That my life at my current home and family was dependent on my performance?

Maybe he just saw my bravado – the playing it cool – and had no idea of the challenges I had to face outside the classroom. And why should I have to be the one to tell him?

Meanwhile, as I was being threatened with exclusion, there were others in my year – the high-performing ones – who were placed in a special group called 'Gifted and Talented'. They were the ones who were expected to smash their GCSEs and potentially go on to university. To boost their aspirations, they were taken on a special trip to Oxford University by the school. I'd asked if I could tag along, but the suggestion was shut down, with the teacher in question looking at me as if I had been smoking a recreational drug.

As exams loomed, I felt as if I had been written off into the bad-breed category. I was seen as a threat and distraction to other students – not as someone with potential.

Day after day, Kelly pored over books at home, ticking off coursework tasks and subject modules. I respected her work ethic. And while Evelyn and

Clinton doted over her diligence, I doubted they were able to see the fears I had on both fronts – at home and at school.

Even Evelyn, with all her warmth and perceptiveness, couldn't really see how my preoccupation with leaving care was beginning to overshadow my day-to-day life. As much as I was cared for, I knew I wasn't as important as Kelly; she was Kelly's proper mum, after all. So I didn't want to bother her with my woes. Instead, just as I'd done at Carmen's and at Roseberry Street, I kept my thoughts to myself. I'd find a way to get by.

Meanwhile, as these new waves of pressure infiltrated my childhood, pre-existing challenges still remained. Being a mixed-race boy, navigating south London brought its own difficulties beyond just being fostered.

After school, I'd get the Tube and then a bus home, with schoolmates Carlos and Andre. Occasionally, we'd also be accompanied by Gabby, a girl in the year below us. She was proper cute. For some reason, I'd do everything during those journeys to try and impress her.

One evening, I got on a packed bus with Gabby. As usual, we sat on the top deck at the back, where I attempted to amaze her with appalling chat and banter.

A few stops into our journey, a bunch of older-looking boys jumped on the bus. They sat around us. I continued with my campaign to impress Gabby.

'Eh, yo. You from Peckham?' one of the boys said to me.

I knew enough to not say yes. Living with Reece and going to the school I did was all the education I needed for street wisdom.

I looked at the boy, doing my utmost to appear confident. 'Nah,' I shot back.

'Why you chatting shit, fam?' he continued.

I ignored him. I could feel Gabby was uncomfortable, as was I.

The boy and his mates edged in and cornered us in our seats. 'What you got for me then, fam?' the boy said to me.

'Ah, nothing.' I was nervous but trying as hard as I could to act unfazed. I still had to keep up a front for Gabby.

'Man will shank you right here and now, you know. Gimme your phone!' the boy said.

I knew enough to not test whether he did or didn't have a knife. I could hear Gabby whimpering but didn't make eye contact with her.

I cautiously drew out my phone, an old Samsung, from my school blazer pocket. I gave it to him reluctantly.

'Pussyhole,' he shouted, taking the phone. Then, as the bus slowed at the next stop, they sped off, calling out insults.

My ego was bruised, but I was relieved. Gabby cried.

'Sorry, Gabby. Are you okay?' I asked her.

'Are you?' she asked.

'Yeah, I'm cool.'

Deep down, I was ashamed for not finding a way to keep my phone and protect my honour, but logic told me there was nothing I could have done. It was a loss that I had to take.

Once the boys had got off the bus, a man turned around to talk to us. 'If you want to cancel the sim on your phone, you can use my phone to call your network provider?' he said, trying to be helpful.

Too little too late, I thought. On that bus, brimming with people, not one person had had the balls to intervene. I vowed to myself, in that moment, that I'd never get mugged again.

I didn't tell Evelyn or Clinton about what happened, but I wished that I had someone to navigate these different terrains of my life with. A dad. A big brother. Someone who could show me what it meant to be a man. Clinton was supportive, but it would have been a stretch to say that I confided in my foster parents. I don't think anyone I grew up with at that time really understood the different facets of insecurity and hardship I had to overcome. Through church, though, I did pick up one thing: I prayed that things would get better. I kept reminding God that, if He was real, I at least needed an invisible father.

Time flew by. My two GCSE years seemed to roll into one.

And with the end of secondary school looming, the reality of leaving care and becoming an adult grew nearer.

With the final year of school came applications for sixth-form, college, higher education or employment.

'What do you want to become?' 'What are your goals?' 'What is your potential?' were the sort of questions now being asked of us during school assemblies. And with those questions and the emphasis on my future came an internal panic. I didn't have the security of parents, or long-term guardians. I didn't have a safety net. While school encouraged us to dream big and get excited about our future prospects, I caved in with despair at the thought of having to live alone at eighteen. My future looked bleak and school didn't understand my needs. While they were banging on about things like university, I was struggling to work out how I'd be able to pay bills and rent all by myself. What I did know, though, is that I'd have Evelyn and Clinton's roof over my head during my exams. I could at least get that far.

With the encouragement of Evelyn and Clinton, I applied to stay on at Bacon's College sixth form and try my hand at A-levels.

'Acceptance depends on your GCSE performance, Ashley. Show us you're serious and we'll give you the chance to remain here,' said the head of sixth form, in response to my enquiry about staying on. Everything – from the home I lived in to my education – seemed to be based on performance. Like the care system, everything was conditional.

While I fretted internally about where my life was going, Kelly bossed this season of life. She was predicted to pass all her GCSEs with flying colours. She had already bagged a bunch of top grades in her earlier exams.

'Ash, you know you can do just as well, yeah?' she said to me once, when we were discussing exams.

'Yeah, I hear you, but I've made so many mistakes at school, you know,' I replied.

'Listen. Examiners don't know about all that. Just smash those exams and your coursework. Forget the past. Look ahead.'

I smiled. That was perhaps the best advice I'd been given. It topped any assembly or lecture from a teacher. Maybe I could draw a line in the sand. Start again and just give it my best shot. Perhaps making an effort at school was worth it, after all. There was something about Kelly's drive that was infectious. She wanted to be a lawyer in the future – well she was definitely persuasive!

Meanwhile, another Christmas was already around the corner, and Evelyn had big plans that year that she wanted me to be part of.

'Now, it's totally up to you where you spend Christmas this year,' Evelyn said, as she sat on the edge of my bed one morning. 'But we are going to Florida in America this Christmas, and we'd love for you come.'

This was a no-brainer. I was going.

Before I knew it, I was on an aeroplane with the Bennetts. This was the most excited I'd ever been about a holiday. Alongside Evelyn, Clinton and Kelly were Diane and Kyan, as well as Evelyn's brother, his wife and their two children.

Where I'd struggled on those foreign trips with Carmen, on this occasion, I felt an innate acceptance. Like I was wanted.

Our flight arrived in Florida late on Christmas eve. We were shattered. Clinton had rented a minibus for the duration of our stay, which we were due to collect at the airport. There was a problem, though, once we got there. They'd run out of vehicles.

After a couple of hours of waiting around for a minibus to be provided, we then drove to another location to collect the keys for our villa.

'I'm sorry, sir. Another group have been assigned your villa. Are you okay to wait while we find you another property? An upgrade, of course,' said the hapless customer service representative.

After another wait, which felt like a lifetime, we arrived at our holiday home during the early hours of Christmas morning. I dashed to my bed and fell asleep instantly.

On Christmas day, during the sunny Florida afternoon, it was decided that we'd go to a local restaurant for lunch. And so, we all assembled in the minibus, kids in the back and Clinton driving.

'So, Ashley, how're you finding your first Christmas with the Bennetts? Chaos?' Evelyn laughed. There were sniggers across the minibus. I smiled.

So far, nothing had gone to plan. For me, though, it was perfect. Throughout all the chaos of sorting vehicles and accommodation, spirits were high. That was until Clinton steered the bus into a side path of sand where a wheel got stuck. The minibus stalled.

Clinton tried to restart the engine. The wheels spun, but the bus didn't move.

'What now?' Evelyn's brother chimed in.

'Let me try again,' said Clinton, huffing.

He revved the engine again. The bus still didn't move.

'All right. That's it. Everyone off the bus,' Clinton demanded in frustration.

In a fit of moans, everyone got off the minibus. The Florida sun beamed down on us. Nothing like your UK Christmas.

Clinton summoned me, Evelyn's brother and his teenage nephew. 'It's Christmas day, so it'll take ages for anyone official to come and help us. So here's the deal, guys. I'm gonna start the engine and I'm gonna need you all to push this blasted minibus out of the sand – you got it?'

We all nodded.

In a flash, we blokes were behind the minibus pushing as Clinton revved the engine. Breaking out in profuse sweat, we pushed for minutes until, finally, we felt the bus gradually shift forward. Clinton eventually swerved the vehicle back on to the road and summoned us all back on. Sighs of relief and laughter filled the minibus.

'Clinton, you've got me all flustered after all of that. Look at you, taking charge!' Evelyn said flirtatiously.

Arriving at the restaurant, we were all ravenous but jovial, despite all the plot twists and disruptions. As I sat in that restaurant with the Bennetts, I looked around at the tired but smiling faces, grateful to have been taken in by this family.

On that Christmas day, as we indulged in a Florida buffet, I forgot about the pressures of leaving care; I forgot about my upcoming exams and the uncertainty of my future. I was, simply, happy.

The holiday flew by. After a stretch of theme parks, US cable TV and good food, we arrived back in the UK for the new year. The descent back into the British January climate brought with it the reminder that I now had just two years left with the Bennetts. Two years left to be a child. Two years before I'd have to leave care.

For the final year of my music GCSE, Mr Tunbridge wasn't my teacher. A more recent arrival was overseeing the most important year of schooling. And where Mr Tunbridge seemed to have brought out the best in me, it wasn't so with Ms Walsh.

Beyond just being a teacher, Mr Tunbridge had made the music room a safe space when I couldn't handle my emotions. He was a pastoral guide. He cared. And whereas he was all about the soul of music, Ms Walsh was more about the theory of it. I can't lie; I didn't like her style.

It was during a composition exercise of hers that I accidentally broke the skin of a drum I was banging. It snapped. I knew she wouldn't be happy. I approached her tentatively.

'Miss, I was banging this drum, and it broke! I swear it was an accident,' I said, as contritely as I could.

Ms Walsh wasn't in the mood. 'Are you aware of how much a snare drum costs? These are a fortune!'

The class went silent, staring on. You know things are getting serious when a music class goes still.

'I didn't mean to, Miss, I promise.'

'Your problem is that you don't think about consequences.'

I could feel my heart beating faster and my temper rearing its head as a wave of embarrassment rose up.

'Ashley, at this point, with exams around the corner, I really shouldn't have to be telling you off about vandalising school equipment . . .' she went on.

I could see there was no use in explaining what happened. 'Do you know what, fuck this,' I protested, walking out of the classroom.

After taking some time to calm down, I went back to my music lesson, but the damage had been done. I had sworn. Caused offence.

'Ashley, please make your way to the headmaster's office. Mr Perry is expecting you.'

I knew there was no point protesting. I slowly walked to the head's office. A sinking feeling of disappointment swirled in my belly. I had lost my temper. Let myself down. I really wanted to be a good student, but I still had those moments where things got the better of me. In moments when I felt judged or unheard, sometimes, I'd lose my cool.

I knew what awaited me in Mr Perry's office. I was on my final warning, and I'd blown it. I'd disrupted a class in the lead-up to GCSE exams. That meant exclusion. No doubt. The breaking of that drum skin would mark the end of my time at Bacon's. I probably wouldn't be able to take my exams, I thought to myself. Where would I end up? That fear of leaving care reared its head again.

Outside Mr Perry's office, I knocked on the door, feeling defeated.

'Come on in, Ashley,' a voice boomed from behind the door.

With my shoulders hunched in disappointment, I walked into Mr Perry's office. Instantly, I saw a letter on his desk with my name on it. I knew my fate. That was a letter of exclusion. What would Evelyn say? What would Helena, my social worker, do?

But just before Mr Perry could utter a word, a sense of indignance rose up in me. 'Sir, I know you're gonna kick me out. I know I've blown it. But I don't wanna leave. Seriously. I promise you, I've been trying. If I go now, I don't know where I'll end up. My foster mum might let me go. I'm sorry! Please gimme another chance.' In desperation, I pleaded with Mr Perry.

Silence.

Mr Perry didn't say a word for what felt like ages. His hand hovered over the letter with my name on it. He appeared to be torn. He looked down at the letter and then back up at me. He breathed deeply.

'Okay, Ashley. One more chance. I don't want to see you here again. This really is your final warning. Now go.'

'Thank you, sir,' I said with a contrite nod.

The moment I left his office, I breathed a deep sigh of relief. I knew there wasn't long to go now until my exams. And I desperately hoped to myself that I could muster up the self-control to make it through the rest of the year.

16

POTENTIAL

In the final weeks leading up to my exams, I decided to take a leaf from Kelly's book. I tried to revise. Weekdays after dinner, I began to sit at the kitchen table, taking notes and memorising facts. It was an alien habit for me. Given the bouts of misbehaviour I'd demonstrated in my final year, I knew I wouldn't get the best grades in my coursework, but at least I could do my best with the limited time I had. Maybe my grades would be good enough to stay on at Bacon's for sixth form.

Finally, the morning of my first exam arrived. I was nervous – perhaps because I actually cared. It was a few weeks of painstaking effort. Apart from one maths exam (where half the students threw their papers in the air and ran out of the hall shouting expletives), it was pretty monotonous and uneventful. But I got to the end of those exams knowing that I'd tried. And given that I wasn't in the Gifted and Talented group, I knew that there was no unrealistic bar of achievement for me. I could take pride in knowing, simply, that I'd sat my exams. Who would've thought when I was a boy living at Roseberry

Street that I'd go on to actually sit all my exams? Myles would have been proud.

I pretty much forgot about my exams once they were completed. All I needed were some middle-level grades to secure my spot at Bacon's. Surely, I must have achieved that, I thought to myself. Hopefully, following Kelly's work ethic had paid off.

The weeks after exams marked the end of the school year and my final at secondary school. Despite having been on the cusp of exclusion, I was relieved to have made it to the end. Back then, our school didn't do proms or anything like that, but we did have a good kickabout in the cages and signed each other's shirts for good luck.

One thing is for sure: if Mr Perry had kicked me out that day, there was no way I would've got my GCSEs. I had never been more grateful for another chance.

Towards the end of the summer holidays, I had to go back to Bacon's to collect my exam results. I had arranged to go in with Andre. His place in the sixth form was already secure. Given the suspensions, mine was dependent on my grades.

Andre and I met up, and as we made our way to our old turf, out of nowhere, nerves suddenly kicked in.

'How you feeling, bro?' I asked him.

'Cool, man. I've been accepted for my A-Level subjects already, so I'm good.'

As we walked up to the school gate, my heartbeat picked up pace. I clearly cared. A lot. When it came to school, this was my chance to prove that I had value;

that I could make something of myself. I wasn't just the care kid.

We entered the reception area where a swarm of kids from our year were hanging around. A range of emotions was evident as people collected their results. As I navigated the school hall, I was greeted by the head of sixth form, Ms Leaf. A short, sprightly, posh lady, she had thick-rimmed glasses and sported a signature bob hairstyle. She looked at me intently.

I was taken aback. Why was she looking at me? And more to the point, why was she smiling? I had never been the object of her attention in this sort of way before.

She ushered me to a corner, away from Andre. 'Well, hello, young man. Ashley. I wanted to give you your results personally.'

My nerves jumped up a notch. 'Why, Miss?' I asked, baffled.

She handed me my results. My hand was quivering as I took the letter. I opened it slowly. Each subject had a letter grade next to it. There was a string of A*s, As and Bs. Two C grades.

I couldn't believe it. I had got a bunch of A*s and As! What the hell . . .

'Ashley, you are one of the highest-achieving students in your year.'

'Hahahaha. Miss – are you joking!' I laughed.

I read and reread the grades again and again. It took me a while to comprehend these results. Just months before, I'd been on the verge of exclusion and now, I had passed my GCSEs with grades far beyond what the teachers had predicted for me. I felt a range of emotions on seeing those grades. But overall, an immense feeling of pride. So much for the Gifted and Talented crew, I thought to myself.

Ms Leaf was beaming. 'You should be really proud, Ashley. And, at Bacon's sixth form, we'd love to help you nurture your academic potential by seeing you through your A-levels. Plus, with grades like these, you should certainly consider applying to a Russell Group university.'

This was the first time any teacher had told me that I had academic potential. This was the hoop I'd had to jump through for approval. In terms of 'Russell Group', I had no idea what she was on about at the time!

Kelly was already home with Evelyn and Clinton when I got back to the Bennetts'. My emotional instinct kicked in the moment I saw Kelly deep in celebration with her parents. It quelled my joy. For all my achievement, I was convinced that my foster parents were less invested in my performance compared to their daughter's. Maybe I was being sensitive, but it was a feeling I couldn't shake. I knew, in that moment, that it wasn't about me or my achievements. It was about Kelly having her moment with her parents, and as much as I longed to break my good news, I had to wait for Kelly to celebrate hers. She was their daughter, after all.

'Kelly, how did you do?' I asked.

'Yeah, smashed it,' she beamed. She had got a bunch of A*s and As.

'Nice one,' I said, smiling.

I wanted the attention to turn to me, but I knew not to demand it. I knew not to take the spotlight off Kelly. I came second in the eyes of her parents. They were delighted with her, and rightly so.

Then Evelyn turned to me. 'And what about you, Ashley? How were your results?'

I showed them my results letter. Evelyn and Clinton glanced at the paper. I thought I saw a flicker of slight shock on their faces.

'Oh, Ashley. This really is great. I am so proud of you,' Evelyn said, hugging me.

I felt awkward, and guilty as Kelly looked on.

'Well, to be fair, if it wasn't for Kelly revising all the time, I definitely wouldn't have tried,' I said deferentially.

That moment of sharing my results with Evelyn and Clinton was a hard one. There was a part of me that wanted unhindered attention, praise and celebration. I wanted to be the son making his parents proud. But at this particular point, I knew beyond a shadow of a doubt, the moment was Kelly's to revel in. Not mine.

I snuck away to my bedroom as Kelly and her parents continued to reflect on her achievements. I glanced at my letter and smiled. Once again, I thought Myles would have been proud.

My exam results weren't the only shock at the end of that summer.

My mum called me with some news. I told her about my grades, but she had a development of her own for me to hear.

'Babe, I've got something to tell you. As you know, things have been going well with Harper. He makes me feel happy . . . safe, you know? Ash – we're getting married!' Mum was crying with joy down the phone.

I didn't say too much. 'Ah, Mum. That's incredible. Congrats!'

I was happy on some level. But I also felt numb to the news. For some reason, I'd often had a subdued reaction to news about Mum's relationship with Harper. These developments just didn't seem to move me in the way that, perhaps, she expected.

Before long – in fact, just weeks after hearing the news – I was in Manchester to be a groomsman at Mum's and Harper's wedding.

Sitting in a pub ahead of the wedding, I couldn't help but notice that no one looked like me. Among the scores of people, there were no other Black or mixed-race faces. Coming from south London and having grown up with Black foster parents, it was hard to ignore just how out of place I felt.

In the town hall, where the ceremony took place, it was clear the majority of guests were on Harper's side. I did my best to represent Mum and her London roots.

To some extent, I felt as if I was on display – there to portray a closeness and connection with my mum that, to me, felt a bit more tenuous. No one asked me about being fostered. Did anyone even know?

Through the ceremony and formalities, I feigned a smile and gave affirming looks to my mum whenever she looked at me. I tried to be 'part of' the day, despite feeling wildly on the margins. I loved my mum. I was glad for her on her special day. But I was still a foster kid. Even though it had now been years since I started seeing her, how close could I say I really was to her? How much could our bond of blood make up for the childhood I'd lived away from her? It was as if the older I got, the more complicated my view of her grew.

But for that day, the wedding, I bore it all with smiles and platitudes. Hopefully, that was enough for her.

Soon enough, the time had come for me to go back to Bacon's College for sixth form and for my A-levels.

If I'd thought being fifteen was a wake-up call to the reality of leaving care, nothing could have prepared me for the year ahead, now that I was sixteen. My social worker, Helena, came to see me at my foster home. After a quick congrats on my exam results, she powered on with her agenda.

'So, you're sixteen now, and we need to come up with some realistic goals for what you want to do once you leave care. We also need to put you on a budget plan because in less than two years now, you'll need to be able to handle money as an independent adult.'

As Helena spoke, she took out some forms – a tick list of priorities to go through with me. This was my leaving-care plan, apparently: goals that we'd achieve by my eighteenth birthday; goals to prepare me for life after foster care.

'Can you cook?' she asked plainly.

'Er, not really.'

She paused and then jotted something down. 'Ooookay,' she muttered while chewing the top of her pen. 'How's your hygiene? Do you wash daily, brush your teeth, etc.?'

'Obviously,' I said, bemused.

'What about money? Do you have a bank account? Savings?'

'Er, I have an account, I think. But I don't think it has money.'

'And what do you want to do after sixth form?' she asked, matter-of-factly.

'I'm not sure . . .' I paused. I was a bit embarrassed to admit it, then said, 'Well, I was thinking about music. But after my GCSE results maybe I could think about uni?'

Helena looked mildly irritated, as if my lack of certainty around aspiration was a nuisance. I hadn't given her a box-tick kind of answer, clearly.

'University could be good. But Ashley, when you turn eighteen, your biggest priority will be paying your bills and rent.' Helena didn't mince her words.

Being hit with this dose of realism was depressing. I wasn't convinced that my genuine aspiration counted for much.

Helena went on. 'You should really think about the financial responsibilities you'll have to carry in maintaining a flat. Would it really be worth racking up all those thousands of pounds in student debt? Do you know what sort of job you'd want after your degree? Practically, would university make sense for you, Ashley?

'Also, Ash, if you were to end up going to university, it'd have to be in London because if you went to a uni outside of London, you'd lose your right to a council flat. You can only get one in the local authority that you're looked after by. It would be impossible for you to maintain student accommodation at a university elsewhere and be able to afford accommodation here in London.'

I respected Helena for being straight-talking, and I knew she meant well, but right then, it was a hard pill to swallow. Each word stifled any emerging ambition I'd gained since getting my exam results, as it felt as if she was talking me out of the idea of uni. Helena didn't deal with blue-sky thinking or possibilities. She was purely practical, even if it meant cutting off the oxygen to any nascent dream of mine. Maybe I was getting ideas above my station as a looked-after child.

As the meeting neared its end, Helena had one final thing to say. 'It's really important that you're able to live on a weekly budget and cook for yourself when you leave. So what I've agreed with Evelyn is that from next week, you'll be given a food budget of £50 a week. With that, you'll have to buy your own groceries and prepare your own meals.' Helena didn't pull her punches.

'So what about Evelyn and Clinton's food?' I asked, a bit perplexed.

'Evelyn can't cook you meals from hereon in, I'm afraid. You'll have to prepare your own dinners and eat them alongside the Bennetts,' she replied.

To me, this felt brutal. I understood the logic behind what Helena was saying, but if I couldn't eat the same meals along with the rest of the family, was I really a part of it? This felt like some form of segregation. And what's more, it felt punitive; a sort of penalty because I was on my way to leaving care.

In the weeks and months that followed, I'd cook my dinner after Evelyn prepared food for the rest of the family. And as they tucked in, I'd begin to throw some ingredients in a pan. While this might have been a necessity when it came to preparing for independence, it chipped away at my sense of belonging at the Bennetts and I couldn't ignore the slight sense of rejection it left.

As I made headway with the first of my two years studying for my four A-levels, I began to lose any of the motivation to study that I'd gained from my GCSE results. It was all because of Helena's leaving-care pep talk and the weekly budgeting exercise, which were revealing to me just how bad I was with money.

The more I was confronted with the prospect of leaving care, the more university seemed to me an unrealistic luxury that I couldn't afford. A degree, I told myself, wasn't going to help me pay for council tax and bills; it wasn't going to help me with the weekly shop once I'd left Evelyn and Clinton's. The grim reality was that I didn't have the bank of Mum and Dad. It also seemed, from what Helena said, that university accommodation would be a cost that I'd never be able to afford.

And with all of that, what was the point of studying? It didn't matter how bright I was, or what potential I possessed. At eighteen, I'd be given the keys to a council flat. I'd no longer be seen as a responsibility of the state. I'd be leaving care. It began to occur to me that, more than anything else, I needed to make money. I needed to survive.

So while mates at sixth form began to talk about higher education plans and employment training opportunities, all I could think about was what it would be like to live alone in a flat. Even at the Bennetts, Kelly began to talk about university and where she could go to get a law degree. My reality was different. How long until I'd run out of food or gas once leaving care? How long would I last in a council flat before being given an eviction notice?

At the young age of sixteen, these were the thoughts that occupied my mind. I couldn't see the significance of A-levels. I was losing sight of my future. I assumed that my late teenage years would be all about getting by.

It was during this time of dwindling expectations that Ms Leaf approached me in the student common room. She summoned me to a corner in her polite but authoritative manner.

'You might find what I'm about to say to you laughable, Ashley, but I have a proposition for you.' She had an air of mystery in her tone. 'Have you heard of the University of Cambridge?' she asked.

My eyes looked up at the ceiling as I considered her question. 'What? That place for posh, rich, clever people?'

'Indeed. There's a bit more to it than that. But yes, that Cambridge University.' She looked at me tentatively and continued. 'Ashley, Cambridge University is one of the best learning institutions in the world. Some of the greatest minds have studied there. They are working with a charity to host a summer school for A-level students from non-traditional backgrounds.'

Ms Leaf paused to see if I was processing where she was going. I needed a bit more, though, because I certainly hadn't ever considered taking a trip to Cambridge, let alone the university.

'Their aim is to host a summer school to give students like you, Ashley, a taster of what it would be like to go to a high-performing university.'

Ms Leaf stopped talking. I was still processing. But I knew for certain that I didn't want anything to do with this poxy summer school.

'No thanks, Miss. Not interested,' I snapped back.

Ms Leaf was immune to my response. 'Ashley, I have already sent in an application on your behalf. If you're successful, I would like you to spend a week of the summer at this Cambridge University summer school.'

What a dicky move. How could this teacher just presume that I'd want to give up a week of my free time to be around some nerds and privileged tosh? She clearly didn't understand the reality I was facing as someone about to leave care. She didn't know that I'd never have the means or support to go to any university, let alone a posh one. There was no point in going to this summer school. She was only giving me the time of day now because I'd surpassed her expectations during my GCSEs, I assumed. I'd been conditioned to think, unfairly now I think about it, that she wasn't encouraging me to go to this school because she genuinely cared about me; she was simply using me to make herself, and the sixth form, look good. I was being used.

'Miss, I'm not really interested,' I said with a tone of lethargy.

'I'll hear none of it! Once I hear back from Cambridge, I'll let you know. And if it helps, I'd be more than happy to speak with your foster carer, social worker – the whole council if needed!' And with that she walked away.

To be fair, I probably wouldn't get accepted, I thought to myself. And what a relief that would be.

My A-level subjects were English, History, Music and Philosophy. Ms Leaf had insisted I take on more of the 'academic' subjects. To be honest, though, I didn't see the use; I kept going back to the recurring thought that university wasn't a possibility, given the looming reality facing me.

As a sixteen-year-old foster kid, I knew that young people who had been in care didn't fare well in higher education and employment, compared to people who hadn't. And while it was never taught to me explicitly, I also became aware of the stigma – the bad reputation that kids like me had in society. In so many of the films and shows I watched, the character of the deranged murderer or violent adversary would always seem to have come from a troubled childhood of foster care. Then there was the way looked-after children were referred to in news media. We were 'the underclass', 'neglected' and 'underprivileged'. Kids like me were seen as the bottom of the pile. The no-hopes.

As I grudgingly went on with my A-levels at the Bennetts', the expectation and hopes for Kelly's future only ramped up. University . . . law school . . . a summer of travel. It was understandable and even inspiring to see how Kelly was flourishing during sixth form. But as time went on, I grew more isolated and fearful in my thoughts of leaving care.

It was against this backdrop, that one spring morning, Ms Leaf once again chased me down in the common room.

'Ashley, you're in! You're in!'

I had been offered a place on the Cambridge Summer School. Ms Leaf was brimming with pride, and I knew there was no way I'd be able to get out of it.

That evening, I shared the news with Clinton and Evelyn. 'I've been invited to go to a summer school at Cambridge University. Um, it's to study history for a week. It's this kind of scheme where they try and get people like me to think about university.'

Maybe I was looking for some show of approval when I told them. They seemed happy. But in my cynicism, I couldn't help but feel that my news could never be anywhere near as important to them as Kelly's.

17

DIFFERENT WORLDS

Not too long after receiving the news about the summer school, I boarded a train at King's Cross Station in London, luggage in hand, making my way to Cambridge.

I found out that Cambridge as a university was collegiate – made up of over thirty colleges – and for the week-long summer school I would stay at a college called Sidney Sussex in the town's centre.

As I walked to the college from the train station, I was instantly struck by the beauty of the city. Beautiful wasn't a word that I would have associated with many of the spaces where I grew up. I loved many parts of south London where I came from – it was my home – but some areas were undeniably neglected by the authorities, even run down. The streets of Cambridge, however, were unlike any I'd grown up on – they were quaint and regal.

On the way to Sidney Sussex, I walked past a university college called Downing College and was captivated by its symmetrical buildings and pillars. These were the types of buildings you saw on postcards, or those posh TV shows. This wasn't how I'd expected Cambridge to look. Although, that said, I didn't have any initial expectations. I didn't even want to be there.

The walk was memorable. The sun was at its peak, kissing the town's river – the River Cam – and the ambience was peaceful and relaxed. When I arrived at Sidney Sussex College, I walked self-consciously through the porter's lodge (basically, a posh term for 'entrance'), where a man in uniform, called a porter, asked for my name. I uttered it quietly, feeling out of place; then, having ticked me off on a list, the porter took me through the college grounds to the room where I'd be staying for the duration of the summer school. I walked behind him, taking in the sandy-coloured buildings, the courtyards and the stunning, lush green-grass quads outside that students were apparently not allowed to walk on. A mixture of both curiosity and imposter syndrome kicked in. I'd never been to a place like this before. It felt foreign. But also, a sense of pride arose, as I thought about the fact that I'd been accepted to spend a week here. Maybe this would be okay, I thought. Maybe Ms Leaf was right in insisting I come.

I arrived at my room. Everything felt luxurious to me. Expensive. Looking out of my window at the college's gardens, I'd never felt so privileged in my life. I guessed that not many foster kids had been in this room before me.

The summer school was made up of dozens of working-class, A-level students from across the country, who studied at state schools and were seen to have performed well academically. I was the only one from Bacon's

College and had no idea who I'd meet or whether I'd get on with anyone.

That evening, all of us summer-school students were to have dinner in the college's dining hall, or 'buttery', as they called it. Once I'd taken some time to process everything and unpack my luggage in my room, I navigated my way over there.

The buttery was filled with long rows of tables and chairs. On the walls were ancient-looking paintings of distinguished historical figures. Swarms of summer-school students filled the hall, all looking for a spot to sit. Glancing around for a seat, I spotted an animated, tall Black boy with a space next to him. For some reason, I hadn't imagined seeing any other Black people. It was a nice relief. I made my way over to the empty seat and introduced myself.

'Hi, mate. I'm Ashley.'

'Yes, mate. Kwame,' he replied with a London accent that instantly made me feel more at home. He immediately felt familiar. We clicked straight away.

'Where in London you from?' he asked.

'South. You?'

'North west.'

Kwame seemed like any boy that I'd grown up knowing. Normal. Same walk of life. That was until he started talking about his interests.

'I'm here for the engineering stream,' he said with a hint of pride.

I looked at him awkwardly not knowing how to react. He continued.

'Bro, mathematics is the one. I love it, man! I'm particularly interested in mechanical engineering. How sick would it be to come here as an undergraduate!' he exclaimed. His eyes lit up with excitement. Wow, Kwame was high on the Cambridge juice. But minutes into meeting him – a Black British-Nigerian boy – and seeing his passion for education . . . well, it blew my mind. How could someone so normal and similar to me have such an interest in things intellectual? I didn't know many blokes from south London who wanted to study engineering at Cambridge, I laughed to myself.

As the buttery filled with excited chatter, I did my best to take in all the conversations and comments from those around me – their interests, backgrounds and aspirations. Most significant to me was how normal many of these people seemed. None of them sounded posh or unrelatable.

As much as I tried to deny it, the vibe in the buttery stirred a sense of enthusiasm inside of me. I was surrounded by kids who were clever, interesting and all seemed to have a drive to do well in life. It was hard to not get a little inspirational kick . . . that was until my mind remembered the inevitable. I would soon be leaving care. No longer looked after. I would soon have to fend for myself.

This world of porters, buteries and Cambridge colleges wasn't for me. I told myself that I'd enjoy the summer school for the week it lasted. It would be nothing more than that.

The next morning, the taster lessons kicked off. I had chosen to do history and so went to the designated lecture hall, where I met a dozen or so other history students. After some polite smiles and platitudes, an older, slender woman with long white hair walked to the front of the hall to address us. She certainly met my expectations of what a Cambridge academic might look like. She seemed both timid and authoritative in equal measure.

'Good morning, I'm Dr Horrox,' she said lightly as her eyes scanned the room. 'I am a Fellow and Director of Studies of History at Fitzwilliam College. My period of specialism is late medieval England – an area that is wildly fascinating once you unpack it.'

Already, students around me were taking copious notes. What was I missing?

I don't think I'd ever come across someone like Dr Horrox before. I don't think I'd ever seen a proper academic. During our hour with her, she spoke loosely about the Black Death of the mid-fourteenth century – the varying accounts communities at the time conjured up to try and explain it and the vast number of deaths.

Even now, I can't explain why, but her presentation captivated me. Her passion, the insight, the authority. My mind was racing, trying to keep up with her every word and idea. I'd never heard of the Black Death before. This woman was an incredible storyteller. I'm not sure I understood a lot of what she was saying or followed it properly, but even the challenge of keeping up with her and grasping her points was admittedly invigorating.

After Dr Horrox finished talking, we were given time to ask questions and make points. I didn't say anything, but my mind was fully alert. It was like mental sport. That's what learning felt like. It felt good.

As I left the lecture hall, rucksack and notepad in hand, a deep sense of pride filled me. The feeling of accomplishment.

Walking through the courts of Sidney Sussex, another history student introduced himself.

'Hi, I'm James.'

'Ashley.'

James had come from a state school in the Midlands, he told me. 'How did you find that lecture?' he asked.

'Yeah, cool. Interesting, I guess. You?' I responded, hiding my enthusiasm. I didn't want to look like a nerd.

'It was absolutely fantastic for me! Dr Rosemary Horrox is a world authority on late medieval history and King Richard III. I've even read a book of hers. I can't believe we just had a lecture from her!' James was beaming.

I admit, I felt a bit thick as James reeled off his knowledge about the woman who had just taught us.

'I don't know about you. My parents took me to visit here when I was four years old,' he went on. 'Ever since, I've wanted to come here. Are you gonna apply to study here as an undergrad?'

'Er, I don't think so. I'm just here to see what it's like,' I said.

Hearing him speak with such passion made me feel a bit despondent. I couldn't relate to him. I'd never known what it felt like to have parents who pushed me. At four, he visited Cambridge with his family. Me? Well, I was new to living at Joyce's. I knew that university wasn't an option for me. I couldn't afford to dream and fantasise about lofty aspirations such as studying full-time at Cambridge. As a result, I just listened to James and smiled. Good for him, I thought.

Before long it was lunchtime. Students across the different subjects were united in the buttery. I found Kwame.

'How was your lesson?' I asked over a plate of food.

'Bro. Seriously. Sick! I defo wanna come here now. I just pray I'm clever enough. I don't know about you, but I am going to apply to Cambridge in a couple of months when the process opens.'

That lunchtime, despite all the enthusiasm around me, all I could think about were Helena's comments. Comments about the responsibility of paying rent, bills and council tax. Why the hell had Ms Leaf sent me here? It was so hard to see everyone's passion, knowing that I, in reality, couldn't really afford to dream big.

At some point in the week, Kwame pressed me yet again: 'So Ash – are you gonna apply to Cambridge?'

'Ah, I don't think so, bro,' I responded.

I didn't want to burden him with the reality of where I was headed. I didn't want to ruin the mood by explaining to him what I was facing now that I was about to leave care. Kwame had determined that he was going to give it a go, so I graciously said, 'I have no doubt you're gonna smash it,' and I wished him the best. Then, in a bid to encourage him further, I added, 'Do it for people like us, bro.'

Soon enough, the summer school came to an end and the time had come for me to make my way back to London. Kwame and I agreed that we'd stay in touch and that he'd keep me posted about his application.

The summer had proved a success. A week in Cambridge, opening myself up to world-class lectures, while still finding opportunities for evening mischief with some of the other students, sparked a new passion for learning – something I couldn't have predicted. And to my own surprise, I was actually going to miss the place. I had never before had the chance to dream about my future, about my potential, in the way I did at Cambridge. At the summer school, I wasn't a looked-after child. Rather, I was a bright kid with a future.

On the train journey back to London, I reflected on the week: the beauty of the city; how enthralled I was at some of the lectures; the self-belief of the other students. I thought about Kwame – this Black guy like me from London – who was full of hope that he would one day go on to study engineering at Cambridge.

And as I sat there in thought, for some reason that I can't explain, a feeling of indignance arose inside of me. *Why* had I decided there was no hope for me after care? *Why* had I given in to the narrative that university wasn't for someone like me? *Why* had I assumed that I couldn't give Cambridge University a chance and at least send in an application? Since when had I come to so blindly accept my fate with social services?

In a moment of self-discovery, on a train back to King's Cross, I determined that I'd at least give Cambridge a shot. It would be hard, but maybe I could find a way to make it work. I didn't know how, but surely, it was worth a go.

It was late evening when I got back to Evelyn and Clinton's.

Evelyn was alone in the kitchen. Still basking in the afterglow of the summer school, I told her about how good it'd been and how it had sparked the belief that university could be for someone like me.

'Evelyn, I think maybe I could apply to Cambridge University for real. To study history,' I said, wide-eyed, in need of affirmation.

She paused and looked back at me with her benevolent smile. 'Ashley, you have just as much potential as anyone else. Go for it,' she said, hugging me.

Maybe it was a bonkers idea. Maybe my new ambition was greater than my ability. Or maybe it was my ego spurring me on because I felt like I had something to prove. Regardless, I'd give it a try.

18

MOBILITY

September arrived, and with it, the second year of A-levels at Bacon's.

I made it a mission to find the head of sixth form, Ms Leaf, instantly. I bumped into her while dashing along a corridor.

'Hi, Miss! The summer school was amazing. I never knew how interesting history could be,' I told her with an unusual enthusiasm.

'Oh, that's wonderful!' she exclaimed.

'Miss, I want to study there, at Cambridge, for a history degree. I want to apply to Cambridge Uni.' I looked at her earnestly.

Her smile dropped. She looked at me. Scrutinised me.

Her tone lowered as she said, 'It is wonderful that we got you into the summer school. But Ashley, going to Cambridge as an undergraduate – well, that's a completely different matter.'

'Miss, I met this historian, Dr Horrox. She said that Cambridge should be accessible to anyone with the ability, regardless of their background. Even a foster kid like me should be able to have a shot,' I said trying to convince her.

I stared at her intently. What was she thinking? What did she see in me? Could she envisage me going somewhere as prestigious as Cambridge? Or did she just see the stigma? The label?

'I have to say, we have never had a student go to Cambridge to study history before. It's very rare that we ever have students make it to Oxford or Cambridge. Ashley, I would need to write you a reference. And I'd have to be honest about your prior suspensions while you were at secondary school.'

For some reason, the faith I had in my aspiration overrode any sense of fear or insecurity. I tried even more to persuade her.

'Ms Leaf, I've never had an ambition before. Would it be okay if I wrote you some history essays – to show you how serious I am?' It was random, sure. But it was an idea. A constructive way to prove to her that I had what it took.

Ms Leaf looked torn. Deep in thought. 'Well, if we were to have you apply to Cambridge, it would be a rigorous process and a lot of work for me and the department. Please feel free to write. In the meantime, I'll have a think.' And with that she dashed off.

Given that it had been Ms Leaf's idea for me to go to the summer school in the first place, I was surprised at how wary she was about my wish to apply. And admittedly, her response did knock my confidence. But to be able to give this application a shot, I knew I'd need to have her on side. I'd need her to sign off applications and give me a reference, as she'd said. Without the support of the sixth form, it would be impossible to send Cambridge an application. As a child, having been shunted across so many foster homes, I'd never trusted or worked to gain the affection of adults – but on this occasion, I knew I had to win Ms Leaf over.

That first term, we were studying Hitler's Germany in history, so I determined that I'd write something about that period for Ms Leaf. Not a piece of coursework, or anything compulsory – I would go above and beyond and write an essay to show her I was serious. A few days later, I dropped the essay off at her office.

At some point during that day, one of the other teachers – Mr Carrigan – approached me, having got wind of my ambition.

'It's great that the summer school gave you a bit of fire for higher education, Ashley. But you must know, applying to somewhere like Cambridge is a lottery,' he said briskly, before walking off just as quickly.

I had no idea what to do with those demoralising words, although what was clear was that Mr Carrigan didn't think I had a chance.

Not long after I'd delivered my essay, however, Ms Leaf pulled me over to a corner of the common room in her characteristic style. Looking at me intently, she said, 'Ashley, I read your essay. Let's sort out that Cambridge application.' Then she walked off.

Result.

When I got home, the whole clan were in the kitchen living space.

I told them about the application and got their full support. Deep down, however, I had no idea if I really had what it took to be accepted by the university. Would I end up being embarrassed in the application process? Was I pursuing something that was genuinely unrealistic, maybe even impossible?

I was also still mindful that I wouldn't be able to afford the cost of going to a university outside of London. How would I even survive the summer, alone in my council flat, in the lead-up to Cambridge? But something inside was compelling me to try. A whisper. And sometimes I'd think back to those words I heard in church while at Carmen's – the words that proclaimed I had purpose . . . meaning.

Maybe my future didn't have to be determined by my start in life. That hope alone was worth me applying to Cambridge.

In the days that followed, I pored over websites and books about Cambridge University. What would it take to study history there? Which colleges should I apply to? How would I account for my suspensions, exclusion and patchy academic performance over the years?

I decided I wanted to apply to the college where Dr Horrox resided – Fitzwilliam College. I told Evelyn.

'Evelyn, Fitzwilliam College have an open day for pro-spective undergrads next Saturday. Can you take me, please? I'd need to go with a parent or guardian.'

Evelyn and Clinton had recently taken Kelly for an open day at the University of Bristol. I still felt I didn't have equal status to her, but was fairly sure they'd support me by taking me to the open day.

Evelyn breathed a deep sigh, leaning over the kitchen sink. 'Ashley, Clinton and I are out then. Would you be okay to take the train up to Cambridge, like you did for the summer school?' she responded.

A feeling of disappointment crept in. I didn't want to be the only student at the open day without a parent or guardian. I didn't want to stick out as the motherless child in that space so soon.

'I just don't want to be the only kid there by myself,' I said, hoping I could sway her.

'I'm sorry, Ashley. I just can't. What about Helena? She may not work on Saturdays, but I can still ask?'

There was no way I wanted to go to a university open day with a social worker. And there was no chance that Helena would give up her Saturday for me. But still, I said, 'Um, okay. If that's the only way I can go. Yeah, please.'

The following day I decided to take it upon myself to ask Helena. I topped up my pay-as-you-go mobile phone with five pounds' worth of credit and called her.

'Hi, Helena, I know you've warned me a lot about how hard it would be to go to a uni outside London, but I really wanna apply to Cambridge. There's an open day for one of the colleges on Saturday . . . can you take me?' I asked cautiously.

Helena's response was unexpectedly short and to the point. 'I'd love to,' she said, and a wave of shock swept through me.

The Saturday of the open day was soon upon us and, with Helena accompanying me, I was making my way to Fitzwilliam College, Cambridge University.

As I nervously walked towards the college's entrance, in among the other visitors, Helena whispered to me, 'I know I've had to talk to you about the harsh realities of leaving care, Ashley, but I will always support you in your aspirations. This open day is a brilliant idea.'

Her comment was as surprising as her willingness to take me to the open day. Behind the veil of her harsh truths and bureaucratic social work duties, she might, it seemed, actually have cared about me doing well. She certainly went up in my estimation, and her words in some way reassured me as we walked through the Fitzwilliam entrance.

Soon after arrival, a student from the college was showing us around the grounds.

Fitzwilliam was different to the college I'd stayed at during the summer school. More modern. A blend of buildings from different eras, with beautiful gardens, it claimed to embody the best of both the old and new of Cambridge University.

'Fitzwilliam has a strong ethos of taking in more students from state-school backgrounds, compared to some of the other Cambridge colleges. We do away with the elitism nonsense of the uni,' the student told us.

Looking around at some of the other prospective students, that seemed hard to believe. Many of them sounded posh to me. Everyone seemed to be with their mums and dads. I was willing to hazard a guess that I was the only foster child there on that open day. Still, I was assured that of all the colleges, this one would be most suited to someone like me.

In the middle of the grounds was a modern-looking lecture hall. We scuttled in there on the direction of our tour guide. And as Helena and I walked in, there stood an authoritative Dr Horrox, in conversation with someone.

'Helena,' I said, under my breath, 'that's the woman who gave our lectures at the summer school.'

'Well, do you want to say hi?' Helena responded.

'Nah, it's cool,' I said dismissively, although I did want to, but just didn't have the confidence.

But then, as if by some sort of sixth sense, she turned around and called me by my full name. 'Ashley John-Baptiste? Oh, hello!' Dr Horrox chirped.

My heart started beating faster. I was bowled over by the fact that she remembered me. I waved and made my way over to her.

'Hello, Dr Horrox. This is my social worker, Helena,' I said, trying to muster my confidence.

'Of course, you are in foster care, aren't you. Well, hello, Helena, welcome!'

She then turned to me again. 'I must say, Ashley, I am really flattered that you've chosen to explore Fitzwilliam as a potential college of choice.'

'Yeah. Your lecture at the summer school was really interesting,' I said, smiling. Then something in me decided to forgo pleasantries, as a wave of boldness that I can't explain overwhelmed me. 'Dr Horrox – I know you have a lot of students to meet today, but I just wanna say, your lecture at that summer school is what made me wanna study history here. Uni isn't something I really thought about until a few months ago. I've made some mistakes throughout school and I know I have a lot of work to do to be ready for Cambridge – but I really hope you'll consider my application when it comes.' I took a deep breath as I finished up: 'I'd really like to come here.'

Dr Horrox's face was inscrutable.

'Well, I am glad you want to study history, Ashley, and I'm glad the summer school helped. You'll be aware, however, that you'll have to apply like everyone else. Good luck!' And with that, Dr Horrox sauntered off, her shawl brushing the ground.

When the open day was done, Helena and I made our way to leave the college, and I took in one more glance of the college grounds. Maybe this would be my last time here, or maybe not. A deep desire burned in that moment. I wanted a shot at life. A chance beyond the grim reality of my childhood. I wanted to make something of myself. I wanted an opportunity to change my life.

On the way back on the train to London, I barely spoke. My mind was consumed with where I had just been. I thought about what it would feel like to be an undergraduate. And I became overwhelmed with a feeling that was all too rare for me – hope.

'So. How did the open day go?' Evelyn asked, as I walked in the house.

I played it down. 'Yeah, cool. Think I'm gonna apply there,' I replied.

'Wonderful,' Evelyn said.

Quite soon after the open day, Ms Leaf cracked on with the application process. Forms were sent to UCAS, she wrote a cover letter and so on. Cambridge University had given applicants the opportunity to explain if there were any personal circumstances that should be taken into account with applications.

'Ashley, I'd like to explain the almost insurmountable challenges you've had to face with moving homes and how, despite all that, you've done so well academically.' Ms Leaf insisted that it was important for Cambridge to consider these circumstances in my application.

I have to admit, it was good having Ms Leaf as an ally in the process and before long, the application was sent. Done. Nothing else I could do. Apparently, it was really hard to get an interview. Only a small percentage of applicants got one. So the wait would be nerve-wracking.

With the application under way, the event of me leaving care loomed ever closer. Every evening I continued to cook my own dinner, separate from the rest of the Bennett family. Kelly's university applications would dominate the conversation at home, and I didn't dare override that with my worries of Cambridge.

With no one to confide in, I kept my thoughts to myself. I had less than a year before my time at the Bennetts would expire. And the more time dragged on, the more focused I became. Getting into university was now my only chance, I thought, to build a life on my terms. I didn't know how it'd all work out – but I knew it had to.

With the hope of going to university, I was now working as hard as I could. I had a legacy of suspension, bravado and getting easily distracted, but I now really began to try. Break times were no longer spent on the football courts or in the common room – but in the library.

'Ash, bro, you all right?' Andre asked one day, clearly concerned

'I'm cool, man. I've just got to work. I've gotta show Ms Leaf I'm serious about Cambridge.' I told him.

'I hear you. I've got your back,' said Andre.

Andre knew more about me than the Bennetts did. He'd known me since I was eleven, living at Carmen's. He'd seen the previous version of me when I lived in the coldness of my former foster home. He was the only person I'd told about the respites and visits with my mum. For all the rejection that I'd encountered, I was glad for his acceptance.

It was during a lesson that Ms Leaf suddenly burst into the classroom, demanding 'Ashley. Come now, please!'

I left the classroom.

'Have you seen your emails?' she asked.

I hadn't.

'Ashley . . . you've been accepted to interview at Cambridge. Congratulations!' she said, clearly stunned.

'Oh my days . . .' I was rendered almost speechless.

For the process, I'd have to do two interviews with multiple academics and send over an essay in the lead-up to the date of the interview. There'd also be a test on the day.

In what seemed like no time, the day had come.

It was a grey autumn day when I walked nervously through Fitzwilliam College in my school uniform, making my way to the candidate waiting room. I was there by myself. Also in the room were a dozen or so other candidates, all accompanied by a parent or guardian; I hadn't bothered asking Evelyn or Clinton to accompany me on this occasion.

I looked around at the other candidates. Mainly white. Posh-sounding. Just different.

As they quietly whispered or asked for the loo on occasion, I noted accents that were different to my own. Some of the other kids were confident-looking. Like they expected to be there and were just waiting for their letter of acceptance. Just glancing at them induced in me an overwhelming sense of anxiety.

I was aware that I didn't really know a lot of history. I hadn't undertaken a lot of interview prep and I wasn't sure what to expect. All I knew was that I'd give it my very best shot. This foster kid from south London would throw his hat in the ring and hope for the best.

After a while, someone called for me.

'Ashley John-Baptiste?'

I put my hand up.

'This way, please.'

I followed behind the polite woman. My heart began to pound. Sweaty palms. A wave of uncontrollable nerves.

I was shown to Dr Horrox's office. I tried to stop the uncontrollable shaking throughout my body. As I was ushered in, I saw Dr Horrox seated on an imposing chair. Next to her was another academic and interviewer, a younger man with a solemn expression. He looked me up and down as I smiled nervously.

I felt way out of my depth in this moment, but it was too late to run away.

'Well, Ashley. Thank you for coming,' Dr Horrox said gently and reassuringly. 'Just take a deep breath. Remember, we're not trying to catch you out here. We just want to get to know you a bit more and get a grasp of your critical thinking.'

They both had pens and notepads. If you took away the countless books that lined the office shelves and the sophisticated accents, this wasn't too dissimilar to a review meeting.

Over the next hour or so, the interviewers grilled me on the essay I'd sent in. Critiqued my arguments. Tore them apart and, ultimately, exposed how inadequate they were. They also asked me impossible questions about a dense piece of text I'd been asked to read moments before the interview. As one fired a question, the other would write ferociously on their notepad. My answers were contradictory at times; there were awkward moments of silence. I'd reach for answers in the fog of my brain when I often didn't have a clue. Dr Horrox's smile from the start of the interview had long since vanished.

And then it was over.

A flush of embarrassment fluttered through me. I looked like a dick. I barely knew what they were talking about for most of that interview. Yet, no matter how stupid I felt, I'd tried to think. Tried to comprehend. Tried to give an answer.

'Ashley, thank you for coming today. You'll hear from us soon. Safe journey home.'

I then had another shockingly woeful interview before leaving Fitzwilliam to make my way home.

Helena called me. 'So how did it go, Ash?' she asked enthusiastically.

'It was crap. Sorry,' I replied and gave a curt reason as to why I couldn't talk.

Back at the Bennetts', I shut myself into my bedroom in disappointment and embarrassment. What a fool I was, I told myself. No one had told me to apply for Cambridge – why had I put myself through that torture? I hadn't answered one question with any confidence or grasp of the subject. Mr Carrigan was wrong: for me, getting into Cambridge wasn't a lottery; it simply wasn't going to happen. Period.

With my dismal Cambridge performance came winter. And as the temperature plummeted, so did my mood and outlook with the inevitability of leaving care drawing ever closer.

Meanwhile, back at Bacon's, students were cementing their plans for higher education or university. Carlos was going to take a gap year, and Andre had a uni in mind that, he said, was looking likely. There seemed to be a pervading excitement among everyone about what their futures held – they carried an enthusiasm to move on.

It was during that term that I turned eighteen. According to Helena, social services had agreed to fund my place at Evelyn's only until the end of my A-levels. From there, I'd have to bid for my council flat. The inevitable was now only around the corner. It was now a matter of months until I'd leave the care system. What a way to kick off the Christmas holidays.

That Christmas was a pleasantly uneventful one spent at the Bennetts. On Christmas day, Evelyn cooked up a storm, the house was filled with family, and laughter seasoned every moment of the day. It was perhaps the most outcast I'd felt at the Bennetts, though. I couldn't escape the fact that it would be my last Christmas there, and I was certain that the following year they'd celebrate Christmas without me and not miss me one bit.

Perhaps the silver lining to Christmas day was that I didn't have to prepare my own meals. I was allowed, I was told, to eat with the rest of the family.

I wondered what Mum was up to. I saw her a couple of times a year; everything else between us was on the phone. She was happily married to Harper. But still, I imagined that Christmas would probably be challenging for her.

As Mum worked to make a new life for herself up north, I struggled with my sense of identity and belonging down in London. The limbo week between Christmas and the new year dragged on until, finally, 2008 came around.

Evelyn and Clinton had gone back to work pretty much at the start of the new year. Kelly and I still had some days to go before the start of our academic terms – days that were filled with trash telly and milling around the local area.

It was on one of the frosty weekday mornings, just before the start of the new term, that I was awoken by the sound of the post being put through the letterbox. It was light outside. Maybe around 9am.

We'd been informed that applicants would receive their acceptance or rejection letters at the start of January, so the sound of post through the letterbox triggered an abnormal level of curiosity in me. Even though I had long since written off the prospect of getting into Cambridge University – I knew I'd flopped the interviews – I still couldn't resist the urge to check the post whenever it arrived.

That morning, I jumped out of my bed and made my way downstairs and through the chill of the hall passageway to retrieve the recently delivered mail. Rummaging through the letters on the floor to check if anything was addressed to me, I saw an A4 envelope with my name on it. Also stamped on the front was the emblem of the University of Cambridge. A sickening swirl of nerves instantly hit my stomach. This was it.

My hand began to tremble as I picked up the envelope and made my way back upstairs to my bedroom. I sat cross-legged on my bed, staring at the letter. Frozen. We had been assured that we'd find out how we did either way, but seeing that letter right in front of me made everything so real. I tried to steel myself. Prepare for the worst.

This application wasn't about Cambridge University entirely. There was something else. Something deeper. This letter represented an opportunity to escape the existence and label of being just another person who'd grown up in care. It was a symbol of who I could become; it suggested to me that I was more than just the difficult start I'd had in life. I wasn't a mistake.

After a while I slowly and carefully unsealed the envelope to read the letter. I didn't need to see a lot of it, just the first few sentences.

Dear Mr John-Baptiste,
Thank you for applying to Fitzwilliam College, The University of Cambridge, for the undergraduate History Tripos . . .

My nerves were palpable. This letter was too drawn out, too long. I skipped a line.

We are delighted to inform you you've been successful in your application . . .

What on earth?
I reread those lines, and the whole letter, numerous times.

Had I misread it? Was this a prank? I gazed at the envelope, checking the postmark and the address of where the letter was sent from. I couldn't believe what I was reading.

And then it began to sink in. The university had given me an offer to study history.

My heart raced even more. I began to jump up and down – quietly, mindful not to wake Kelly, who was still asleep.

There I was – a mixed-race foster boy, from south London, in his foster home, reading a letter of acceptance from Cambridge University. I had written this off. I hadn't believed it was possible for me.

In a fit of joy, I ran to Kelly's bedroom. I had to tell someone.

'Kelly!' I shouted outside her door.

'What?' she asked, still half asleep.

'Cambridge University have given me an offer. I got in!' I exclaimed.

She opened the door, smiling. 'Seriously, Ashley. That's mad. Absolutely incredible. Aah . . . Congratulations!' She gave me a warm hug.

I ran around the house, beaming. Then I wondered about Kwame, the boy from the summer school. I dashed downstairs to the house phone and dialled his number with shaking fingers, then waited for him to pick up.

'Ashley?'

I tried to calm my voice. 'You good, Kwame? I'm just wondering about Cambridge. Have they got in touch?'

Kwame went uncomfortably quiet for what seemed like ages. 'Bro . . .' he said.

'What?' I asked.

'Cambridge gave me an offer,' he said.

'Aaaarggghhh,' I screamed, jumping up and down with the house phone in my hand. 'Bro, well, listen to this . . .' I continued. 'Cambridge have accepted me, too – to study history!'

Kwame shouted back in equal measure.

'Bro, so you *did* apply?!'

The joy that was exchanged during that phone call is hard to describe. And in those moments of jubilation, I forgot that I was soon to leave care, forgot about the real pressures that awaited once I left the Bennetts. I was in a moment of pure pride and delight. I had actually achieved something.

That evening, I told Evelyn and Clinton and was met with hugs and celebration. Maybe they were proud, I thought to myself. And even if it wasn't the pride of real parents, pleasing them was well worth it.

As for when I told my mum on the phone – she cried in pure joy. Hearing her reaction, I knew the news had brought a sense of redemption for her, too.

What I wasn't prepared for, however, was the affirmation I received when I went back to Bacon's for the start of term. Every teacher in sight congratulated me – even the ones I didn't know. And it wasn't long before I saw Ms Leaf rushing down a hallway towards me in absolute thrills.

'We did it, Ashley! We did it! Well done!' She was as happy as I had been the day I found out.

Previously, teachers had shouted at me about incidents and suspensions. Now there were shouts of praise. This was wild.

Mr Tunbridge made a point of finding me to say well done. My mind ran back to when I would go to his music room as an escape. And then there was Mr Perry – my headteacher who had been on the verge of excluding me. I had never been more grateful for another chance. Had he kicked me out of Bacon's, I wouldn't have got my GCSEs or just got an offer from Cambridge.

It felt deeply rewarding to be celebrated for once. I was showing the world around me that there was more to me than just being care experienced. I had talent. Ability. Of course, once the celebrations calmed down, it would be time to deal with reality and knuckle down to some hard work. After all, I had yet to get the grades. But, for the first time, I had a vision – and that became a source of motivation.

19

BIRTHRIGHT

Perhaps I could've stomached the pressure if my only responsibility from then on was to work for good A-level results. Truth be told, however, that wasn't even the half of it.

Not long after starting back at sixth form came another review meeting with the social work professionals. And the top line was clear: if I accepted my Cambridge offer, I would have to forfeit the council flat I was eligible for in London.

'Ashley, the local authority cannot financially support you with both Cambridge student accommodation and your London council flat. It's one or the other. If you decide to go to Cambridge, you'll have to live in Cambridge during the holidays, too, and rely on a student loan and employment to fund you. We can't just throw around public money, Ashley,' Helena said matter-of-factly.

'But I won't be able to live in my student room during the holidays. They don't allow it. And I want to have a home to come back to, like other people,' I said in frustration. Was I asking for – expecting – too much?

'Well then, your other option, potentially, would be to stay in halls at Cambridge during termtime, and then, for the holidays, we can move you between hostels in London, until you graduate?' Helena suggested, trying to find a point for optimism.

No one in the review meeting seemed to acknowledge the significance of this Cambridge achievement and what it could mean for other looked-after children in the area. No one seemed to view it as a positive thing. Rather, it appeared that this opportunity was presenting Helena and the local authority with difficulties they now had to address.

Truth is, if I was a young offender or lived in a care home, I would have cost social services far more money. Surely providing support into university shouldn't have been so much hassle. Wasn't the point of the care system to get young people to positive places of achievement like university? Wasn't the system meant to care?

A feeling of frustration rose up inside me. 'I'm not gonna lie,' I said bluntly. 'It feels like my achievement is a bit of an inconvenience to your flipping bureaucracy and the social work boxes you wanna put us care kids into. All you guys are doing is presenting me with all the problems and reasons why Cambridge may not be a good idea. Why it can't work. Do you want me to go or not? Surely, as social workers you're meant to have the solutions and push me to do well, to reach for the stars? It seems you're more concerned with me being able to pay bills and meet the requirements of all your forms than you are with me fulfilling genuine life potential.' I stopped talking. My breathing was heavy.

I knew that Helena genuinely cared, but that she also had council rules and strict guidance to follow, especially when it came to resources. Today, she was toeing the party line.

'Well, there is another potential solution,' Helena said tentatively. 'The resources do dry up when a young person reaches eighteen, but maybe Evelyn and Clinton could take you for the holidays if you end up going to Cambridge?' Helena suggested. I looked at both Evelyn and Clinton.

'We'd love to. But the council would need to support us. We don't have the money,' Evelyn said frankly.

My stomach plummeted. I knew the Bennetts didn't owe me anything – they'd already done more than enough in taking me in – but part of me hoped that they'd see me as their child and decide that, regardless of the cost, they'd have me stay with them throughout university. They didn't see me as that, though. Staying wasn't an option.

I'd thought that particular review would be positive. A celebration of sorts. But instead, I was given a month to come up with a decision about university and accommodation. By the look of it, Cambridge was turning out to be an impossible prospect.

A couple of weeks later, at Bacon's, Ms Leaf informed me that the local MP, some bloke called Simon Hughes, would be visiting our sixth form. I didn't see what that had to do with me, but she went on: 'In light of your

Cambridge news, Ashley, you'd be a fantastic ambassador for the college. Would you be willing to give him a tour of the sixth-form facilities?'

I wasn't used to being the golden kid – the one being handed all the prissy opportunities. It all made me feel a little uncomfortable; I just wanted to be one of the normal boys, not a teacher's pet. That said, I knew I didn't really have a choice in the matter.

And so, days later, there I was, giving Mr Hughes a tour of the college. I didn't know much about party politics then. He was, apparently, a Liberal Democrat, but I didn't know how to engage in conversation with politicians and I was nervous. By the time we met, though, he had already got wind of my Cambridge offer. It wasn't normal for Bacon's to have students go to Oxbridge, and as a result, word had got around.

'So, mister, how are you feeling about Cambridge?' he asked.

I didn't really feel up to conversation, especially about university. The chances of actually being able to go were growing ever smaller given all the limitations I'd have to deal with after leaving care. But then a thought occurred to me. An idea. Simon Hughes was my local MP. He had some level of power and influence in the local area. Maybe – just maybe – he could help me.

I decided I'd take a shot and ask for his help. I spoke frankly. 'Mr Hughes. I'm not sure if I'll be able to go Cambridge. I am a foster child. When I leave care, I am supposed to get a council flat, but I've been told by the local authority that if I choose to go to Cambridge,

I'll forfeit my right to a council property in the area. Apparently, I can't have a London base while living in Cambridge for the academic year. Can you do anything to help?'

Simon Hughes paused in his tracks, deep in thought. He then looked at me and said, 'I am so sorry this is what you've been told. I want to help. Could you please email my constituency office and, from there, I will make some further enquiries.'

'Okay, thanks,' I responded, my heart leaping with excitement.

I did email Mr Hughes's office and, weeks later, he arranged for me, Evelyn, Clinton and Helena to meet up with a rich lawyer in the local area who was keen on hosting me during the holidays.

So it was that on a dark February evening, we found ourselves outside the man's London town house. The building towered above me as I looked up at it. Growing up in south London I'd seen posh houses like this but had never been in one.

We were met by an elderly white couple. 'Hello. We are the Cramptons,' said the man, greeting us warmly and gesturing to his wife. 'Welcome, indeed!' Tall, with thick-rimmed glasses and long, flowing white hair in a ponytail, the man was called Jeremy. His wife, Holly, was shorter, friendly, but clearly more reserved.

Inside the house, an ornate flight of stairs swirled upwards for at least two floors, it appeared. We were shown into a massive living area with high ceilings, walls covered in expensive-looking artwork and luxurious ornaments scattered around the room. The Cramptons didn't have kids and the house was spotless, with none of the buzz and noise of the Bennetts' home.

Jeremy had built a glittering career as a solicitor. He also did other bits in the local area. Sat on boards and community groups. Things that liberal, middle-class people did. Holly had worked in the civil service or something like that, but she was now retired.

Walking around their beautiful home, it was hard not to be intimidated by the sense of privilege they exuded. I found most adults unrelatable at the best of times, but this couple seemed to be worlds apart from anything I'd known before.

We took it all in. I didn't know what to say, but Jeremy soon struck up a conversation.

'So, Ashley. Simon Hughes says you've been offered a spot at Cambridge?'

'Yeah. I have,' I replied. I felt like I was being vetted for a new foster home.

Then Helena chipped in. 'So how would things work if Ashley was to spend the holidays here as a uni student, Jeremy?'

'Well, it's a matter of what's convenient for you, Ashley,' he said, as if the question was redundant and the answer obvious. It became apparent quite quickly that he wasn't one for being under scrutiny. He went on, 'Ashley, let's show you our spare room, where you'd likely stay if you were to live here.'

We were led up the stairs to the top of the house and into a snug bedroom with a double bed and en-suite bathroom. Towels and bedclothes were folded on a chest of drawers and a flat screen TV perched in one corner.

'This is so nice,' I remarked.

'Well, Ashley – it's yours if you want it! For as long as you're at uni, you can stay here and come and go as you please,' Jeremy said.

On hearing those words, a sense of relief kicked in. I would be able to go to Cambridge, after all.

'Seriously, Jeremy and Holly. Thanks so much. I really appreciate it,' I said with gratitude and humility.

We chatted a bit more, then we left their home, making our way back along that lovely, upper-class London street. Evelyn and Clinton hadn't said much during the visit. Maybe they knew that where I went to stay after leaving their place had nothing to do with them.

I was kind of inspired by Jeremy and Holly's house and certainly grateful for the offer they'd extended, but at the same time, I felt unsettled. Why were they taking me in? Was it some sort of middle-class guilt? Would I have my own freedom in their home? There were too many ifs for me to feel entirely comfortable.

Before Helena parted ways with me and the Bennetts that evening, she had one more bit of info for me.

'Well, Ashley. If the offer from Jeremy and Holly wasn't enough for you, the local authority has now also agreed to pay the rent at your London-based council property if you do indeed decide to go to Cambridge.'

I had to pause to take in the news. This was big and so unexpected. It meant I now had a decision to make. Would I stay with Jeremy and Holly? Or would I take up the offer of a council flat? As I made my way home with Evelyn and Clinton, a satisfying feeling of relief and achievement kicked in. Relief at the fact that I'd used my voice and spoken up to my local MP. And a sense of achievement in that I'd found the courage to not take no for an answer. That day I was learning a lesson: that I was more powerful – more capable – than I'd ever been taught or shown.

Within a matter of days of our visit to Jeremy and Holly's place I had contacted Helena to say that I'd decided to take up the offer of a council flat. I wanted to leave care. I no longer wanted to live in the homes of strangers, trying to be worthy of their benevolence and generosity. I'd move into my council flat, pay my way and do everything I could to rebuild my life away from the shadows of my past.

For once, I felt like I was able to look forward to my future. And as spring eventually loomed on the horizon, so did the hope of what was to come.

The time that so many of us sixth formers had been dreading finally arrived: our A-level exams. That was enough to dampen any joy I had encountered in securing my council-flat accommodation post-care. And while exam woes were the dominant downer for other students, I grew ever more fearful about the reality of moving into a council flat.

In the lead-up to exams, I still had to cook my own meals and handle my weekly budget. It was tough love, I told myself. And, as for during my exams – well, I had to bid for a council flat and think about how I would use the small budget given to me by social services to buy modest furnishings for my new home.

In many ways, my examinations were peripheral to the responsibility of preparing for leaving care. But the exam season was also underpinned by another emotional upheaval: every exam I took reminded me that I was getting closer to leaving the Bennetts. Helena's word was final. I'd leave the Bennetts once I'd finished my exams. I knew I'd miss them – miss the sense of love and family.

So as Kelly ranted in the evenings about exams, I would fret about the prospect of living alone. Yet, despite my inner fears, the demands of exams ploughed on, and in among the emotional weight of all I was forced to think about, I tried to approach my exams in the best way possible.

After a month and a bit of sitting exams and being preoccupied with all that lay ahead, I had sat my last paper. And as my mates and fellow students erupted in elation over the end of exams, I cowered in fear at my looming reality.

20

A MAN NOW

I wasn't ready to leave Evelyn and Clinton's. I knew it deep inside. The independent cooking, budgeting plan and review meetings weren't enough to prepare me for living alone. Despite having turned eighteen, I still felt like a child.

The local authority had secured me a council flat of my choosing based on the properties available, and now my exams were over it was a matter of days until I'd move in. Evelyn took me to Ikea to get some basics – dining bits and the like.

I held no sense of optimism for the summer break. It would be a season of sorting out my flat, trying to make ends meet and living alone – all stuff that filled me with dread.

Evelyn and Clinton allowed me to eat with them for my final days as their foster son. They kept conversations light and attempted to maintain the laughter that was so typical of their home. But for me, I couldn't escape the imminent. The inevitable. I was soon to leave care. All alone.

I was that boy once again being told that I was leaving Joyce's. Crushed, feeling that same rejection and aloneness. Regardless of the home I lived in, the people I got to know, their benevolent words, I always arrived back at the same question: who really cared? Yet I had been through moments like this several times throughout my childhood. I knew how to put on a front, to show no vulnerability.

Over those days, I thanked the family. I was grateful. Grateful that they had provided me a route out of Carmen's, grateful that while I was there, they at least tried to care. Maybe they weren't the family I wanted, or even needed, but at least they were something. They had helped me. I suppose I was better because of them.

On the afternoon I was due to leave, I packed my luggage and the bits I had accumulated for my flat. Kelly and Clinton said their goodbyes with heartfelt hugs and helped me load my luggage into Evelyn's car. Clinton was the only foster dad I'd ever had; Kelly the only foster sister.

In those final moments at the Bennett house, I thought about Evelyn's wider family: her brother and his family who I'd gone on holiday with. I thought about her grandson, Kyan, and her other daughter, Diane. I thought about the mates I'd made in the local area and the way I'd fallen in love with the music and community at Evelyn's church. I didn't get to say bye to all of that, to all those people.

Even though I had started again on a number of occasions, it never got easier. In those final moments, I could still feel the sense of optimism I experienced when I had first moved in. But with it were lingering questions. I wanted to ask the Bennetts straight out, to their faces, why they couldn't keep me on – but I couldn't muster the forthrightness back then.

For one last time, I took in the surroundings of the Bennetts' home. For one last time, I stood in my bedroom, looked at my bed. Wondered if they'd take in another foster child to fill it.

Then, soon enough, I was in the car with Evelyn and, after one last wave, we were off to my flat.

There was a finality but also an informality to parting with Evelyn.

I knew it was the end of my time as her foster son, but she had said she loved me, that her door was open and that I could visit the family any time. On the surface, those were lovely words, but they also put me in a quandary. They placed me in a grey area. Was I like a son or not? If she loved me, why couldn't she support me through university? Being turfed out into a council flat, alone, didn't particularly feel like love. But I didn't voice any of this. I just took Evelyn's words on board and thanked her. As I had told myself in so many other situations as a looked-after child, I should only ever be grateful.

We soon turned on to the road where my flat was. A residential street with terraced houses dotted on either side of a large council housing estate that towered above everything else. From a distance, the design looked like a large, bricked ship.

My flat was in a smaller compound. We slowly parked up. I took deep breaths. Took a beat. A weird sense of peace filled me as I considered the building I was about to enter. This moment had crept up on me. All the meetings and warnings couldn't have prepared me for this moment of being here by the kerb, outside my council flat.

Evelyn rubbed my back gently, handing me the keys to my new home.

I was silent.

Getting out of the car, a warm breeze brushed me. The sun was still lowering in the evening summer sky.

As I walked toward the building, Evelyn followed behind. A fob got me through the first door. I walked up a small staircase and spotted the door to my flat. On the door was a sticker, presumably put there by the previous inhabitant. It read: 'Glory to glory'. Was this a sign? Would I go on to glory? Would things get better for me? Did I have a future to be hopeful for?

For the first time, I unlocked the door to my flat.

I walked through a small passageway. One bedroom, a living room, kitchen and bathroom. There was a small cupboard for the gas and electric – devices that were, at this point, foreign to me. The flat looked on to a nice green backdrop through the living room window.

The property was mostly empty, but the kitchen had a small fridge and washing machine, put in by social services, I guessed. In the bedroom was a bedframe without a mattress.

Evelyn helped me unload my luggage, which soon filled the living room. And once all the luggage was in the flat, Evelyn took her cue to leave.

'You will be absolutely fine. And if you need anything, I'm a call away. Take care, dear.'

We embraced in a parting hug and then she left. And that was it. She was no longer my foster mother. She was relieved of any responsibility for the eighteen-year-old she once used to look after.

With the door closed behind her, a silence ensued. I double-checked to make sure the door was locked. Then I slowly walked around the place, inspecting it. I couldn't quite believe this was my home.

In a matter of moments, I'd thrown off my clothes and laid out the single mattress that Evelyn had got me on the living room floor. I collapsed on to it, surrounded by the clutter of my possessions.

It was now dark outside; I didn't have any living room curtains at that point. And in that dark and silence, I wrestled with my thoughts. Was I safe? What were my neighbours like? Would I survive alone?

And before long, I'd crashed out to sleep.

It took me a good few minutes to establish where I was when I woke up the next morning. It was a lovely day – clear skies, sunlight – but sitting up on my mattress, as I looked around the living room, it still felt foreign and I experienced an inescapable sense of anxiety. It was now on me to work everything out. I was in charge.

I was entitled to a fifty-quid weekly allowance and housing benefit. My rent and council tax would only be funded by the local authority once I started the university term, and my first allowance hadn't arrived in my account by the time I moved in, so I used some of the remainder of my 'furniture payment' to get some groceries. I strolled around the local streets, looking for a corner shop or grocery store. I had to remember my keys, I told myself – there'd be no one to let me in if I forgot them.

Once I'd got food for the next few days I went back to my flat. At the Bennetts' I had embedded myself into their way of life. Now I was free to set my own culture; find my own rhythm.

The silence was deafening around the flat. I hooked up my iPod speaker and set up the keyboard. Looking at my luggage and the empty spaces around the house, I didn't know where to start.

One of the positives to where I now lived was that Andre from Bacon's lived fairly nearby. He popped over. 'Bro, your own place, you know!' he exclaimed. He was far more excited than I was. He helped me distribute my luggage and possessions into the correct rooms. He didn't say a lot. Didn't verbally acknowledge the clear pressure I was under, but his actions told me all I needed to know. He was with me. He had my back.

In that first week or so at my flat, I relied on Andre like a brother. At some point, we bought some plastic chairs and a small telly to fill a corner of the living room. He also brought a couple of others over to help me paint the walls. For those first few days, it was music, decorating and friendship, signed off each night with a Chinese takeaway. Maybe not the healthiest, but there was an

enjoyment in those first few days that I hadn't antici-
pated. Many teens, when they finish college, head off on
summer trips or festivals; for me and a small crew of
friends, it was about making this council flat a home.

At some point during those first few days, my allowance finally cleared into my account. I gradually learned
the ropes of utilities, updated my address with the bank
and tried to find some flow for being an adult. On the
nights when I was alone, I'd play my keyboard, grasping
for the peace that I often lacked.

My first proper week at the flat brought with it a visit
from Helena.

'Hiya, Ash,' she said as I welcomed her into my flat.

She made herself very welcome, trotting around the
rooms, inspecting, checking my cleanliness, peering into
the fridge and more.

'So how's it been moving in?' she asked.

'Yeah, all right, I guess. A few friends have helped me
settle in,' I said.

'Well, this is a lovely start. And over time, as you
budget, you can buy more bits of furniture,' she pointed
out reassuringly. 'Are you ready for Cambridge?' she
then asked.

Since moving into the flat I hadn't given any thought
to university. I still needed to get my predicted A-level
grades to secure my spot, and then I needed to wait
for my student loan to buy the necessary bits for my
course.

'Luckily, I don't start until October. But once my student loan comes, I can start getting the stuff I need.'

Looking at me, she paused and then changed gear. 'Now that you have officially left care, Ashley, I will no longer be your social worker. You'll still have some oversight by the local authority. You will be given what's called a personal advisor. Basically, someone who will check up on you every now and then for a couple of years. But really, Ashley, it's over to you now.'

Helena had a way of hitting me with a dose of reality. I knew she meant well, though.

'Thanks for being my social worker. And thanks for taking me to see Cambridge,' I said gratefully.

We chatted a bit more, then Helena said her final goodbye. And, just like that, another social worker was gone. There'd be no more reviews; no more regular visits. To be honest, there were elements of the social worker offering that I was glad to see the back of.

As the weeks of the summer progressed, there was only so much spending time with mates and busying myself in decorating that I could do before a looming sense of isolation kicked in. I struggled to live on my weekly allowance. I had to decline nights out, embarrassed to admit to friends that I was broke and, often, I had to forgo proper meals.

I can still remember one Saturday, a month or so into being at the flat. I had spent my last. I had less than a pound – literally pennies (perhaps I had bought one too many Chinese takeaways that week). I rummaged around the kitchen cupboards, looking for ingredients to make dinner. I found some pasta and an onion. I then made my way to the local off-licence, hoping I'd be able to afford a tin of tuna.

Once there, I found the tinned food section and spotted the tuna. I counted my pennies, desperately hoping I could afford a tin. Unfortunately not. I was twenty pence or so short. I left the shop downcast. There was no way I'd lose my pride by asking the shop owner to let me off. So I went back to my flat. And, as evening sunlight pierced through every window, I made a serving of pasta and onion for dinner and ate alone.

My next instalment of allowance wouldn't come through until Monday, and I had no idea how I'd get through Sunday. That said, Saturday had enough worries of its own.

To my relief, I had smashed my A-levels and secured my place at Cambridge. But with the drowning responsibilities of my new flat, it hardly felt like an event worth celebrating. I told my mum on the phone and some friends – but I had no family to celebrate with in person. I brought the news back to my flat. Alone.

With my university place now confirmed, I was unable to find a short-term job for the interim. I had no choice but to see out the summer on my meagre allowance and pray that my student loan would hit my account on time.

Since moving into my flat, I hadn't heard from the Bennetts much. I didn't want to look needy by calling them, and I suppose in the absence of me calling, they didn't feel the need to call me. Maybe they wanted to but thought it appropriate to give me space. Or maybe they weren't thinking about me at all. I had no clue. Either way, it made me feel that they no longer felt responsible for me.

Some looked-after children wholeheartedly looked forward to living independently. But that summer of moving into my flat, as I awaited the start of Cambridge, felt like weeks of solitary attrition. I was just about getting by.

Social services eventually bought some of my course books for university ahead of me getting my student loan. And in among all the hardship, the odd Cambridge letter would come through with updates about the start of term.

As time came to consider the start of term at university, I thought about how I'd get there with my luggage. I imagined that the other freshers would be going with their families – I knew Kwame was being driven up by his mum.

I didn't want to go to Cambridge for the start of term alone. I didn't want to stand out. I called up Evelyn.

'Hi, Ashley. How's it going?' she asked brightly.

'Good, thanks.' I felt vulnerable, nervous, given what I was about to ask her. 'Evelyn – I hope you don't mind me asking . . . do you reckon I could get a drive up to Cambridge for the start of term, at the beginning of October? Or maybe Clinton could take me if you're busy?' I asked with some trepidation. I didn't have it in me to tell her I wanted a lift to make it appear to other freshers that I had a family; so that I could appear normal and fit in.

'I know you've had a lot of settling in to do, Ashley. And I'm sorry, but we're taking Kelly to her university around that time and we can't do both. Call us once you're there, though!' Evelyn was clearly letting me down as gently as possible. But I couldn't help but feel that she had washed her hands of me. Not in a bad or brutal way. More pragmatic. Her time as my foster carer had ended and it felt like she no longer saw it as her job to support me. Fair play.

I determined that I'd be fine on the train. If I was able to survive the summer, I'd find a way to get to my university.

In what seemed like no time, the morning came for me to make my way up to Cambridge.

With two full cases and a rucksack, I navigated bus-tling streets and buses to make it to King's Cross Station. I collected my pre-paid ticket, frantically searched for the right platform. Dishevelled and sweating profusely, I lugged my stuff on to the train and clamoured aboard, breathless. I grabbed a seat. Sitting down, I took a beat and regulated my breathing.

A summer out of care had been enough to tell me that I wasn't prepared for adulthood. I had struggled to make ends meet, was still lacking essential bits for my new home and, most of all, I felt as if I'd spent months in solitary confinement. Living with the Bennetts had at least meant there was always noise to drown out the silence of loneliness. That summer, however, I had been forced to confront the reality of my abandonment. Leaving care had exposed me to just how alone I was.

Sitting there on that train, though, as it pulled out of the station, I realised that I had got through it all. Despite all the homes I'd been turfed between, all the suspensions and my primary school exclusion, I was about to start a degree at the University of Cambridge. As crap and as tired as I felt, I was about to embark on a new beginning.

I tried to imagine what awaited me at Cambridge – what sort of future could I pave for myself? Who could I become? Yet as much as my mind pondered all the potential ahead of me on that train journey, it kept going back to Myles.

The thought of Myles soothed my anxiety. I hadn't seen him for about a decade, but there he was at the forefront of my thoughts as I made my way to Cambridge. I wondered what he might be up to in that moment; what young person he might've been cajoling into doing better.

If not for Myles, I wouldn't have been on that train. If he hadn't got me into Galleywall School, I wouldn't have had the chance to learn. As distant as he was, his impact on my life was still tangible. And as I looked out of the train window and allowed myself to finally wander in hope for all that lay ahead, I looked back fondly – only wishing I had a chance to thank Myles for the path he unwittingly set me on.

ACKNOWLEDGEMENTS

This book has been two years in the making and without the backing of my family, it just wouldn't have been possible.

To my wife, Joanna John-Baptiste, thank you for your undying support. Thanks for listening to me all those countless evenings when I'd pop into the living room and recite some past moment I was writing about. I couldn't have done this without you.

To my daughters, Zoe and Mia. In years to come you may read this book. I hope you know how much of an antidote to the trauma of my childhood you have been. Your love and joy uplifts me daily. I love you. Because of you both, I have a happier and richer life.

A big thanks to the team at Hodder. Rupert, you have been an incredible editor. I appreciate your sensitivity and patience. I am thoroughly grateful for your oversight. Kimberley, thanks for all you've done in helping to promote this book. You are a talent and I, for one, am excited for your future.

Thanks to my literary agent, Jim Gill. Thanks for seeing the potential in this book and helping me craft the proposal. I also have to thank Jo Carlton – the most reassuring and supportive agent. Your integrity is as evident as your brilliance. Here's to many more years working together.

Thanks to BBC News for granting me the permission to write and publish this book whilst being a member of staff.

I want to acknowledge every care-experienced person reading his book. We are not a homogenous herd – we come from different walks of life and have varying experiences of being looked after. That said, I hope this book resonates with you. I hope my story, in some way, encourages you on your journey. You are not alone.

And to every reader,

Thank you.